STAAR Grade 5 Science Assessment Secrets

Study Guide
Your Key to Exam Success

STAAR Test Review for the
State of Texas Assessments of Academic Readiness

Dear Future Exam Success Story:

Congratulations on your purchase of our study guide. Our goal in writing our study guide was to cover the content on the test, as well as provide insight into typical test taking mistakes and how to overcome them.

Standardized tests are a key component of being successful, which only increases the importance of doing well in the high-pressure high-stakes environment of test day. How well you do on this test will have a significant impact on your future- and we have the research and practical advice to help you execute on test day.

The product you're reading now is designed to exploit weaknesses in the test itself, and help you avoid the most common errors test takers frequently make.

How to use this study guide

We don't want to waste your time. Our study guide is fast-paced and fluff-free. We suggest going through it a number of times, as repetition is an important part of learning new information and concepts.

First, read through the study guide completely to get a feel for the content and organization. Read the general success strategies first, and then proceed to the content sections. Each tip has been carefully selected for its effectiveness.

Second, read through the study guide again, and take notes in the margins and highlight those sections where you may have a particular weakness.

Finally, bring the manual with you on test day and study it before the exam begins.

Your success is our success

We would be delighted to hear about your success. Send us an email and tell us your story. Thanks for your business and we wish you continued success-

Sincerely,

Mometrix Test Preparation Team

TABLE OF CONTENTS

Matter and Energy

Classical states of matter

The three classical states of matter are solids, liquids, and gases. Solids have a definite volume and density at a given temperature and pressure, a degree of structural rigidity and a constant shape, and a resistance to flow. However, some solids such as modeling clay can flow and undergo deformation under pressure. Liquids also have a definite volume and density at a given temperature and pressure, but they flow readily and do assume the shape of their container. However, a liquid will only occupy the portion of a container that is equal to its volume. A gas is far more diffuse than even a liquid, and will expand to fill the entire volume of its container. The molecules are spread much farther apart, and they move more rapidly and randomly than in a liquid.

Atom

A neutral atom consists of an extremely dense nucleus composed of one or more positively charged protons and (except for hydrogen-1) a varying number of uncharged neutrons. The nucleus is surrounded by a cloud of one or more negatively charged electrons that are equal in number to the protons in the nucleus. The protons and neutrons are bound together by the strong nuclear force, which is stronger than the repulsive force between the positively charged protons. The negatively charged electrons are attracted to the positively charged protons by the electromagnetic force. The number of protons determines the identity of the chemical element, while the number of electrons in the outermost shell determines the ways in which the atom interacts chemically with other atoms or molecules.

Molecule

A molecule is an electrically neutral combination of two or more atoms joined by covalent bonds. Molecules can be as simple as diatomic hydrogen or oxygen (H_2 and O_2) gas or water (H_2O), or as complex as large biochemical macromolecules such as proteins, starches, and cellulose. Ions (electrically charged atoms that have unequal numbers of protons and electrons) are joined by ionic bonds, and are not considered molecules. An example of an ion is simple table salt. Metals are not considered molecules either. They consist of positively charged ions that are in a sea of unattached and unlocalized electrons.

Chemical

A chemical compound consists of two or more different elements with a fixed ratio of atoms. These atoms are held in a specific arrangement by covalent, ionic, or metallic bonds. Substances formed from two or more atoms of a single element are not considered compounds. Examples are diatomic hydrogen, oxygen, nitrogen, and chlorine (H_2, O_2, N_2, Cl_2) or polyatomic molecules such as O_3 (ozone), P_4, and S_8. An example of a compound is when two hydrogen atoms and one oxygen atom combine to form water (H_2O). Other examples of compounds include: two hydrogen atoms, one sulfur atom, and four oxygen atoms combine to form sulfuric acid (H_2SO_4); two oxygen atoms and a carbon atom come together to make carbon dioxide (CO_2); and four hydrogen atoms and a carbon atom combine to form methane (CH_4).

Archimedes' principle

Ships and other floating objects made of materials that are denser than water float because of the empty space they contain inside their hulls. A ship weighing 5,000 tons overall will displace 5,000 tons of water, but this weight of water will occupy a smaller volume than the ship itself. Once this amount of water has been displaced the ship will not sink any deeper into the water and will float. Archimedes' principle states that the buoyant force is equal to the weight of the water (or any other fluid displaced). The reason a solid piece of iron or a rock sinks is that it weighs more than the volume of water it displaces. For the same reason, because a helium-filled balloon is lighter than air it will rise until the air's density is reduced such that the volume of air displaced is the same as the volume of the balloon.

Intensive and extensive physical properties of matter

Intensive properties are those that do not depend upon the size of the sample. Examples are density, melting-freezing point, boiling point, color, chemical reactivity, luster, malleability, and electrical conductivity. Extensive properties do depend on the size of the sample. Examples include the amount of space occupied (volume), mass, and weight. Note that mass and weight are not the same thing. Mass is the amount of material present in a body, whereas weight is the gravitational force acting upon that mass in a specific gravitational field. A 100-kilogram object has the same mass on Earth as on the Moon, but its weight will change markedly. It will weigh 980.7 Newtons (220.5 pounds) here on Earth, but only 163.5 N (36.75 lbs) on the Moon. In outer space this object would weigh nothing at all, but would still have a mass of 100 kg.

Physical changes

Physical changes are those that do not affect the chemical properties of a substance. Changes in state are physical changes. For example, a liquid can freeze into a solid or boil into a gas, but its chemical nature remains the same. Ice, steam, and liquid water are all still water (H_2O). Physical properties include features such as shape, texture, size, color, odor, volume, mass, and density, although some changes in color or odor can indicate chemical changes. Certain changes such as the dissolution of ionic or polar compounds in a solvent are considered physical changes even though they involve breaking chemical bonds. If a saltwater solution evaporates, crystalline table salt will be left behind as a precipitate; adding water will produce a new saltwater solution.

Chemical changes

Chemical changes occur when chemical bonds are broken and new ones are formed. The original substances are transformed into new compounds or elements, and energy is released or absorbed. For example, methane can combine with oxygen to produce carbon dioxide, water, and energy: $CH_4 + 2O_2 \rightarrow CO_2 + 2H_2O +$ energy. Similarly, an acid (sulfuric acid) and a base (sodium hydroxide) can combine chemically to form a salt (sodium sulfate) plus water: $2\ NaOH + H_2SO_4 \rightarrow 2H_2O + Na_2SO_4$. The rusting of iron (oxidation) is a chemical change, as is the decomposition of water into oxygen and hydrogen when an electric current passes through the water: $2H_2O +$ electricity $\rightarrow 2H_2 + O_2$. In each case, the original compounds or elements (reactants) are transformed into new compounds (products) that were not originally present.

Force, Motion, and Energy

Heat transfer

Heat transfer occurs through radiation, conduction, and/or convection. Radiation transfers heat energy by electromagnetic waves, and is how solar energy is transported across the vacuum of space from the Sun to Earth. The other two forms of heat transfer involve particle motion in physical media. Conduction transfers heat energy through collisions between adjacent particles. As molecules gain heat they acquire more kinetic energy and move faster. When they collide with neighboring particles, some of this kinetic energy is transferred, which causes the neighboring particles to begin to move faster. Some substances such as metals are much better conductors of heat than others, such as down, which has numerous empty air spaces. Convection occurs when the flow of a warm fluid carries heated material from one place to another. This is seen in boiling water and the convection currents in the atmosphere or Earth's mantle.

The following is a diagram showing the three major ways heat is transferred:

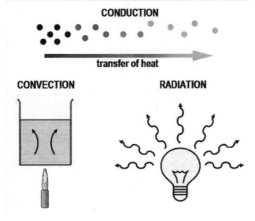

Electrical circuit

An electrical circuit is a closed path within which electrons can flow from a power source (a battery or alternator) through a conducting medium such as an insulated copper wire (or salt water) to a load (such as an incandescent light or other electrical appliance) and back to the power source or "ground." When the connections are complete, the current flows. When they are broken (such as when a switch is turned off), the current ceases to flow. Electrical current can do work against the circuit's resistance to the current flow, including the resistance of the copper wire and the mechanical and other resistance in the appliance (e.g. the amount of heat necessary to make a metal filament in an appliance glow and emit light).

Refraction

Refraction is the reason why a straight stick appears bent when part of it is submerged in water. Light travels in a straight line until it enters a transparent medium with a different index of refraction. In empty space, light travels at a speed very close to 3×10^8 m/s (300 million meters per second). Whenever it enters a transparent medium that is denser than

- 4 -

the one it was traveling in, it slows down and is refracted (bent). The index of refraction is calculated using the formula $n = c/v$, where c is the speed of light in a vacuum and v is its speed in the new medium. Some indices of refraction are: space, 1.00; air, 1.0002926; water at 20 °C, 1.33335; and glass, 1.51714. The denser the transparent medium, the more the light slows down and the more it bends.

Light traveling through the air slows down and is bent as it passes through a glass window pane. When it reaches the other side of the glass, it immediately resumes its original speed and direction.

Light passing through a prism

White light is what we see when all of the colors in the visible spectrum are present in the right proportions. It is the color of the light produced by our Sun, incandescent and fluorescent lamps, and white-emitting light-emitting diodes (LEDs). When white light passes through a prism it is separated into its component colors. For humans, the visible color spectrum ranges from violet through blue, green, yellow, orange, and red. Humans see electromagnetic wavelengths from about 390–570 nanometers, corresponding to frequencies of 400–790 trillion cycles per second (terahertz). Longer wavelengths and lower frequencies have lower energies than shorter wavelengths and higher frequencies. They also scatter less and travel farther in transparent media (such as air or water). Light from the setting Sun has farther to travel through air than when it is higher in the sky. Red light penetrates better than the other colors and so sunsets appear red.

Geological weathering and erosion

All rocks, minerals, and soils are subject to the forces of weathering and erosion. Weathering is the mechanical and/or chemical breakdown of rock by liquid water, wind, ice, snow, temperature changes, and the biological actions of organisms. Erosion involves the breakdown, movement, and transportation of parent rock and soil by water, wind, ice, or simple gravity. Water erodes bedrock by both mechanical and chemical processes:

alternate freezing and thawing cracks rocks (frost wedging or frost heaving), carbonic acid formed by CO_2 dissolved in water chemically dissolves limestone and other susceptible rocks, and salts and other minerals may precipitate out as new minerals. Mass wasting involves the downslope movement of soil and rocks due to gravity. Lichens and mosses create a humid environment and also directly attack rocks chemically, and many burrowing and tunneling organisms hasten the breakdown of soil.

Potential and kinetic energy

Potential energy is stored energy that can be released to do work. Kinetic energy is "energy in motion" that actively performs work within or against a system. For example, if you carry a basketball up a flight of stairs against the fc
gravitational energy in the ball as potential e......gy. .. y ou .... stairs, that energy is released as kinetic energy, which can knock over a glass of milk or other object that happens to be in its way.

Newton's Third Law of Motion

Newton's Third Law states that every action has an equal and opposite reaction. Whenever you push on an object (exert an action) such as a wall, for example, the wall pushes back directly against you with exactly the same force (the reaction). That equal and opposite force exerted by the wall against your hands and arms is the resistance you feel. As long as your action and the wall's reaction are balanced, no net force is exerted and neither you nor the wall move: $\vec{F}_1 = -\vec{F}_2$. However, if the "wall" is a flimsy bamboo curtain, you can easily push it aside or knock it over. The bamboo curtain's inertia is not adequate to counteract the force you applied. A net unbalanced force acts against it, which causes it to accelerate (move). Now, Newton's Second Law applies. This law is expressed with the formula $\vec{F}_{net} = ma$, which states that force equals mass times acceleration.

Newton's Second Law of Motion

Newton's Second Law states that the force operating on a body is equal to the body's mass times its acceleration: $F = ma$. It applies to situations in which there is a net unbalanced force. If the net applied force is sufficient to overcome the body's inertial and frictional forces of resistance, the body will accelerate (change its direction and/or speed of motion). The degree of acceleration will be directly proportional to the applied force and inversely proportional to the body's mass. This is shown graphically below.

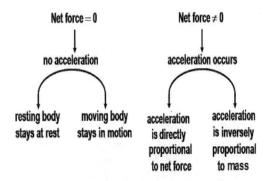

E = mc²

This is Einstein's famous equation showing the equivalence between energy and matter. E is the amount of energy in a system, m is its mass equivalent, and c is a constant: the speed of light in a vacuum (3×10^8 m/s, or 300 million meters per second). This is the basis for the atomic bomb. A huge amount of energy can be released by converting a very small amount of matter multiplied by the speed of light squared: 9×10^{16} m²/s². As an example, one kilogram of matter can be converted into 9×10^{16} kg m²/s², which is equal to 90,000 trillion joules. This is the explosive equivalent of 21.5 megatons of TNT.

Earth and Space

Igneous, sedimentary, and metamorphic rocks

Igneous rock forms when hot magma or lava cools beneath or above the ground, respectively, to form large- or fine-grained crystalline, porous, or glassy rocks of varying chemical compositions. Sedimentary rocks form from previously weathered (eroded) parent rock, which itself may be igneous, sedimentary, or metamorphic. This weathered material deposits out in layers and eventually becomes compacted and/or chemically solidified into sedimentary rock. Sedimentary rocks can also form as coal or as limestone or dolomite from the heating and compaction of calcareous exoskeletons of aquatic animals and algae. Sediments can also form as salt deposits from evaporating water bodies. Metamorphic rocks are altered, partially re-melted, and generally highly crystalline igneous, sedimentary, or even older metamorphic rocks that have undergone various degrees of heating and compression. Heat from volcanic sills and dikes can produce contact metamorphism in immediately adjacent rock, while uplifting mountain ranges result in large-scale regional metamorphism.

Fossils

Fossils are the preserved traces, casts, or mineralized remains of animals, plants, and other organisms that lived tens of thousands, millions, or even billions of years ago. Preserved remains younger than about 10,000 years are not generally considered fossils, but there is no particularly good reason for this other than convention. Most fossils are mineralized hard parts such as teeth, bones, and shells that were buried. The organic material was gradually replaced, molecule by molecule, with minerals. Therefore, the structural details are preserved. In some cases, soft objects such as feathers and leaves and delicate creatures such as insects and spiders were buried in mud, where their detailed casts were preserved. They may also have been trapped in tree sap and fossilized intact in amber. The sedimentary environments and strata in which fossils are found reveal a great deal about the habitats and environments of the preserved plants and organisms. Many fossils can be accurately dated by radiometric means.

Climate and weather

Climate refers to the more or less stable, usually regional (as opposed to worldwide) statistical patterns of temperature; humidity; type (rainfall, snow, ice) and timing of precipitation; amount of frost, sunshine, and clouds; prevalence, direction, and speed of winds; seasonal patterns (including the prevalence and types of storms and severe weather); and other atmospheric and meteorological phenomena over many decades to hundreds, thousands, or even millions of years. Climate is influenced by latitude and longitude, altitude, geography, and the presence of nearby mountain ranges or large bodies of water such as the Great Lakes or oceans. Climate can also apply to the planet as a whole when referring to time periods such as glacial epochs ("ice ages"). Conversely, weather is the short-term (days, weeks, months) variation in meteorological conditions in a given region.

Cooler temperatures at higher altitudes

As altitude increases there is less atmosphere pressing down upon the surface. The area 62 miles above Earth's surface is generally regarded as the boundary between Earth's atmosphere and space. The average atmospheric pressure at sea level is 1 atmosphere: 14.7 psi = 760 mm Hg (760 torr). At the same temperature and humidity this is reduced to 10.1 psi (526 torr) at an altitude of 10,000 feet. When the pressure on a gas is reduced it expands and cools adiabatically (i.e. without exchanging any heat with the surrounding air mass). As the gas molecules expand they exert work against the surrounding atmosphere to push it aside. They lose kinetic energy as a result and the temperature drops. Conversely, increased pressure exerts work against the gas molecules, causing them to gain kinetic energy (move faster) and heat up. This is why it is generally warmer at lower elevations and cooler at higher ones.

Tornado

A tornado is a violent and dangerous rotating column of air that usually extends from a severe thunderstorm to contact Earth's surface (either land or water). Tornadoes can occur almost anywhere in the world (except Antarctica), but the most common and dangerous ones occur in the United States east of the Rocky Mountains. The rotating column is invisible until an observable funnel forms from condensed water droplets and/or it picks up dust and debris from the ground. The extreme rotating wind speeds markedly reduce pressure inside the funnel (Bernoulli's principle). The expanding air molecules inside this low-pressure vortex cause the temperature to drop (just like a deflating balloon gets colder) until water vapor condenses into visible droplets, forming a condensation funnel. An F0 tornado on the Fujita scale has wind speeds of 40–72 mph and causes only minor damage. The most violent (and fortunately very rare) F5 tornados can have wind speeds as high as 318 mph and can cause catastrophic damage and loss of life.

Earth, Moon, and Sun

Earth is the third planet from the Sun. It orbits the Sun once every 365.256 days. A solar year is therefore 6 hours longer than 365 days, which is why an extra day is added to the calendar year every four years. In a leap year, February has an extra day and the year is 366 days long. Earth rotates on its axis approximately once every 24 hours, constituting a day. The Moon rotates in synch with Earth, meaning it turns on its axis once in the time it takes to orbit Earth. Therefore, the same side of the Moon is always visible to viewers on Earth; humans did not see the far side of the Moon until manned spacecraft orbited it.

Earth and Moon sizes and distance
The diameter of the Moon is slightly more than one quarter that of Earth. The average distance between them is about 385,000 kilometers (60 times the radius of Earth), although it varies from approximately 362,500 (356,400–370,400) kilometers at perigee (its closest approach) to about 405,400 (404,000–406,700) kilometers at apogee (its farthest distance from Earth). If Earth were the size of a quarter, the Moon would be about 6¼ feet (1.9 meters) away. The following graphic shows the relative sizes of Earth and the Moon and their average distance from each other.

Renewable and nonrenewable resources

Renewable sources of energy include solar, wind, tidal, and geothermal resources. These can be tapped essentially without limit. Nonrenewable energy resources include coal, oil, natural gas, and other "fossil fuels." Once these are mined they cannot be replaced. Minerals are not renewable, at least not on a time scale that works for human societies. Timber harvested for lumber, wild fish stocks, and aquatic food resources other than fish are renewable if they are properly managed and not overexploited to the point that they cannot replace themselves.

Water cycle

The water cycle is the complex movement of water molecules in the form of liquid water, ice, and water vapor above, on, and within Earth, and from one area to another. Water can evaporate from the ocean to the atmosphere and condense out again as liquid rain, ice, or snow to fall on land, rivers, lakes, or the ocean. Water can be taken up by plant roots and transpired into the air from the leaves. The total amount of water on Earth remains roughly the same, but it constantly changes states (from liquid, to solid, to gas) as it moves from one place to another in the air, via ocean currents, or through other processes.

Plate tectonics

Earthquakes result from the movement of a dozen or so major lithospheric (crustal) plates that float upon Earth's mantle (asthenosphere). These plates move about each other in response to complex convection cells set in motion by Earth's interior heat. Two plates move apart from each other at divergent boundaries, or spreading centers, and come together at convergent boundaries. When thin, denser, iron- and magnesium- rich oceanic crust collides with thicker, lighter, silica-rich continental crust, the former is subducted beneath the latter. The subducted material carries scraped-off continental crust and seawater down with it. As this material melts, it rises as a mixture of magma and steam to produce explosive volcanic mountain ranges such as those surrounding the Pacific Ocean Basin. When two continental plates collide at convergent boundaries, the crust buckles and thrusts up massive mountain ranges such as the Alps and Himalayas.

Earthquakes

Earthquakes result when an amount of energy large enough to cause a noticeable movement of the ground is suddenly released. This can be due to sudden slippage along faults, crustal plate boundaries, or at mid-oceanic seafloor spreading zones when the accumulated stress (potential energy) from plate tectonic movement is suddenly released as kinetic energy. A combination of upwelling convection currents in the mantle at seafloor spreading zones and tensile forces pulling the plates apart under their own weight at subduction zones cause oceanic plates to move relative to one another. This in turn causes collateral stresses along faults and other zones of lithospheric weakness. Large sections of crust become locked in place because of friction as the stresses accumulate. When the accumulated stress is sufficient to overcome this friction, a sudden slippage occurs, generating earthquakes. Earthquakes can also be caused by volcanic activity, massive landslides, nuclear explosions, and other events.

Solar System

Our solar system consists of the Sun and the eight major planets that orbit it. Arranged in order from the closest to the farthest from the Sun, these planets are: Mercury, Venus, Earth, Mars, Jupiter, Saturn, Uranus, and Neptune. Between Mars and Jupiter lies the asteroid belt of small, rocky objects of varying sizes. Pluto is no longer considered a planet, and is now classified as one of the five known trans-Neptunian objects regarded as minor planets. The Kuiper Belt extends from Neptune at 30 astronomical units [1 AU (the mean distance from the Sun to Earth) is 150 million km] out to about 50 AU, or 1 light-year (~9.5 trillion kilometers) from the Sun. It contains countless numbers of icy bodies of water, methane, and ammonia, some with rocky cores. Beyond the Kuiper Belt lies the hypothesized spherical Oort Cloud, thought to be the source of long-period comets.

Milky Way Galaxy

The Milky Way Galaxy is a giant spiral galaxy with a diameter of 100,000 light years (about 946 thousand trillion kilometers). Recent evidence suggests that the Milky Way has a central bar, and may therefore have to be reclassified as a "barred spiral" or intermediate type galaxy. It contains between 100 and 400 billion (most likely about 200 billion) stars, and is one of roughly 200 billion galaxies in the known Universe. It is home to our Sun and its Solar System, which is located about 26,000 light years (~246 thousand trillion km, or a little over halfway out) from the galactic center. Like the galaxy's size, the exact distance is not known because of clouds of gas and dust that obscure our view. Our Solar System rotates around the galactic center about once every 250 million years.

Life cycle of a star

Stars are formed when enormous clouds of interstellar molecular gas (primarily hydrogen and helium) and dust collapse under their own gravitational attraction. As the molecular cloud collapses, its pressure increases and it heats up to form an ionized gas (plasma). Eventually, it will reach core temperatures of between 4 million kelvins (K) for a small star and 40 million K for a massive star. These temperatures drive hydrogen atoms together so that they fuse and form helium. Some of the matter contained in the four hydrogen atoms is lost as energy, which prevents further gravitational collapse of the star. Depending on its mass, the star will continue to shine for several million years (very massive stars) to 10 billion years (our Sun) or even longer. Most stars will go on to form other elements later in their life cycle until they begin to synthesize iron. At that point no energy is released and, depending on its remaining mass, the star will collapse into a white dwarf, a neutron star, or a black hole.

Light year

A light year (ly) is the distance light will travel in a vacuum in one year. It is a common measure of astronomical distances. Since light travels in empty space at 300 million meters per second, the distance it will travel in one year is equal to:

$$\frac{3 \times 10^8 m}{1\,s} \times \frac{1\,km}{10^3 m} \times \frac{60\,s}{1\,min} \times \frac{60\,min}{1\,hr} \times \frac{24\,hr}{1\,day} \times \frac{365\,day}{1\,yr} = 9.46 \times 10^{12} \frac{km}{yr}$$

This is close to 9.5 trillion kilometers in a year (about 5.9 trillion miles per year). It should be noted that a light year is a unit of distance, not time. Another astronomical measure of distance is the parsec, which equals about 3.26 light years, or approximately 31 trillion kilometers.

Organisms and Environments

Ecosystem

An ecosystem is a large or relatively small biological community, which consists of interacting groups of organisms of various species (plants, animals, fungi, etc.), as well as the physical environment, the climate, and the community's location in space and time. Each ecosystem has its characteristic groups of primary producers (photosynthesizers), primary and secondary consumers, predators, prey species, parasites, and decomposers. A community may be a small microcommunity of all the organisms in a single creosote bush or a vast assemblage of organisms in a biome spanning the better part of a continent. These biomes may include a tropical rain forest, temperate deciduous forest, taiga, grassland, chaparral, desert, tundra, or one of several major aquatic biomes. Regardless of its size, a given community will have numerous characteristic species.

Flow of solar energy through ecosystems

About 30 percent of the total energy from the Sun that reaches the Earth is reflected back into space. Of the remaining 70 percent, one-third is absorbed by clouds and two-thirds make it to Earth's surface (land and water), where it drives weather patterns and ocean currents. Most of this energy is ultimately radiated back into space. Less than 1 percent is actually available to be used by plants and other primary producers for photosynthesis. Of the solar energy that reaches the producers, 90 percent is lost as heat, and only about 1 percent is used to produce sugars. Animals that eat plants use only about 1 percent of the energy they consume; the rest is lost as heat. Likewise, predators feeding on primary consumers and decomposers can only absorb and use 1 percent of the energy they take in. The number of steps in this chain must be limited for there to be sufficient solar energy to sustain life.

Carbon dioxide-oxygen cycle

Photosynthetic plants and algae take in carbon dioxide (CO_2) from the air, which is converted into 3-carbon sugar compounds. During photosynthesis, a water molecule (H_2O) is split, and oxygen gas (O_2) is given off as a waste product. Animals, plants, fungi, algae, and other organisms that engage in cellular respiration break down the sugars produced by photosynthesis and use the oxygen produced by green plants to produce energy in the form of ATP molecules. In addition to energy, cellular respiration produces O_2 and H_2O as waste products, which are then used by primary producers (photosynthetic organisms) to produce sugars.

Photosynthesis

Photosynthesis is the process by which chlorophyll-containing autotrophs use the energy in sunlight to convert carbon dioxide and water into carbohydrates and release oxygen as a waste product. The general reaction is $2nCO_2 + 2nH_2O + h\nu(\text{photons}) \rightarrow 2(CH_2O)_n + 2nO_2$. The process involves two stages, which are known as the light and dark reactions. In the light reactions, photons provide the energy to split a water molecule. The electrons released are boosted into higher energy states and allowed to "flow downhill" (energetically speaking) to generate reducing equivalents—protons (H$^+$) and/or electrons (e$^-$)—and the energy-carrying molecule ATP. In the dark reactions, atmospheric CO_2 is captured and converted by the reducing equivalents and ATP into a 3-carbon sugar: PGAL. This PGAL is usually later converted into 6-carbon sugar phosphates, and then into sucrose, starch, and cellulose.

Adaptations of marine vertebrates

Sharks, porpoises, and extinct ichthyosaurs all separately and independently developed elongated, fusiform (spindle-shaped or torpedo-like) streamlined body forms, one or more erect dorsal fins, swimming flippers, and powerful swimming tails. All have somewhat similar outward appearances, but these animals are unrelated. Their similar appearance is the result of convergent evolution—the adaptive development of similar shapes in response to shared environments and predatory lifestyles. Sharks are cartilaginous fishes that breathe with gills, ichthyosaurs were air-breathing marine reptiles, and porpoises are air-breathing mammals whose ancestors lived on land.

Innate and learned behavior

Innate, or instinctive, behavior includes actions that are programmed by an animal's genes. It is behavior that is elicited automatically in response to environmental or social cues. It is not based on prior experience or learning. Examples include marine turtle hatchlings automatically moving toward the ocean and safety. Learned behavior must be taught by more experienced mentors; it is acquired through learning. Examples include many territorial songs sung by male songbirds, which must be taught. Different populations of the same species of songbird sing slightly different songs (dialects). Similarly, in the 1930s and 1940s in England, birds known as Great Tits learned to open milk bottles that were delivered to people's doorsteps and drink the milk. This behavior was learned and passed along by inexperienced birds watching experienced birds, and the behavior spread quickly throughout the country. Likewise, bears in national parks have learned to associate humans with food, which has caused major conflicts and problems in these areas.

Metamorphosis in insects

Nearly all insects undergo metamorphosis—a distinct change in form from their immature to adult stages. Many insects such as grasshoppers exhibit incomplete metamorphosis, in which the nymphs or juveniles resemble miniature adults but lack certain adult structures such as wings and genitalia. These insects undergo a series of growth stages known as instars, each of which is followed by a molt. Immature insects that exhibit complete metamorphosis are called larvae. At some point, these larvae spin a cocoon around themselves and become inactive pupae or chrysalides. After a time, they emerge as fully-formed adults. Butterflies, bees, and wasps are all examples of insects that undergo complete metamorphosis.

Scientific Investigation and Reasoning Skills

Scientific method

Scientists investigate natural phenomena by completing the following steps: (1) making observations and recording facts and data, (2) formulating a hypothesis or plausible explanation for the data, (3) making one or more predictions based on the hypothesis about what might happen (if x is true, then y must follow), (4) conducting one or more experiments to test whether the hypothesis holds up or must be rejected, and (5) forming a conclusion based on the experimental outcome. To be credible, hypotheses must be consistent with the rest of scientific knowledge. No limit exists as to the creativity that may be involved in a scientific investigation. However, most experiments involve a test, experimental group of things, or organism, as well as a single variable to be tested. There is also a control group, which is treated exactly the same as the test group; the only thing that is altered is the single variable being studied. If the experiment fails to support the hypothesis, it must be at least provisionally rejected.

Temperature scales

The three main temperature scales are Fahrenheit, Celsius, and Absolute, or Kelvin. The first is used mainly in the United States, while the Celsius scale is used in the rest of the world and in science. The Absolute scale is used almost exclusively by scientists. The following formulas can be used to convert temperatures from Fahrenheit to Celsius, and from Celsius to Fahrenheit:

$$°C = {}^5\!/_9(°F - 32); \quad °F = {}^9\!/_5(°C) + 32$$

The Absolute scale is based on the Celsius scale. One kelvin (one K) is equal to one degree Celsius. The difference is that zero is set at absolute zero (= -273.15 °C) instead of at the freezing point of water. Absolute zero is the temperature at which all atomic and molecular motion stops and matter as we understand it would cease to exist. This temperature can never be reached in the real world, although scientists have come within a few billionths of a degree of reaching it in the laboratory. Even in outer space, the microwave background radiation has a temperature of 2.725 K (-270.425 °C).

The following is a diagram comparing the three temperature scales:

Conversion example
Convert absolute zero into degrees Fahrenheit:

$0 \text{ K} = -273.15 \,^\circ\text{C}$; $^\circ\text{F} = \,^9/_5(^\circ\text{C}) + 32 = \,^9/_5(-273.15 \,^\circ\text{C}) + 32 = -459.67\,^\circ\text{F}$

Mercury thermometer

Elemental mercury is an ideal thermometer material. At a given pressure, it evenly and reversibly expands when heated and contracts when cooled. A fixed amount of mercury is sealed inside an evacuated tube and a calibrated temperature scale is attached. This scale is calibrated by fixing the boiling (100 °C or 212 °F) and freezing (0 °C or 32°F) points of water at 1 standard atmosphere of pressure (760 mm Hg). The distance between these two points is divided using 100 or 180 evenly spaced lines, depending on whether the temperature will be measured in Celsius or Fahrenheit. These divisions are continued above and below these points to expand the scale above boiling and below freezing. As the mercury heats up it expands at a constant linear rate and its volume increases uniformly. The mercury column rises and falls in the tube according to the temperature, which can be read directly from the attached scale.

Balancing a chemical reaction (equation)

For an equation to be balanced, both sides must have the same number of atoms of each element. Reactants appear on the left side of the equation and products appear on the right. The elements are balanced by placing the necessary coefficients in front of each element or compound. In a simple example, diatomic (molecular) hydrogen combines with diatomic oxygen to form water: $H_2 + O_2 \rightarrow H_2O$. Adding up all the atoms shows that the left side has one more atom of oxygen than the right. Since water contains twice as many hydrogen atoms as oxygen atoms, placing the coefficient 2 in front of both the hydrogen molecule on the left and the water molecule on the right balances the equation: $2H_2 + O_2 \rightarrow 2H_2O$. There are 4 hydrogen and 2 oxygen atoms on both sides of the balanced equation.

Practice Test

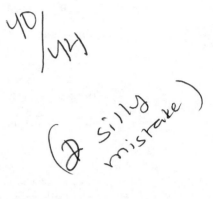

1. In a science experiment, a student is asked to identify the freezing and melting points of water. Which piece of laboratory equipment should be used?

Ⓐ Balance

Ⓑ Thermometer

Ⓒ Ruler

Ⓓ Graduated cylinder

2. In the diagram shown below, four wheels are in contact such that each wheel turns the opposite direction from the wheels it is touching. Wheel A is being turned clockwise by a force as shown. Which statement about wheel D is correct?

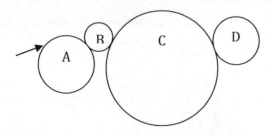

Ⓐ Wheel D does not turn at all because there are too many wheels between it and wheel A

Ⓑ Wheel D does not turn at all because it is not touching wheel C

Ⓒ Wheel D turns counterclockwise

Ⓓ Wheel D turns clockwise

- 17 -

3. The United States is divided into four time zones. The east coast is three hours ahead of the west coast. This means that when it is 6:00pm in New York, on the east coast, it is 3:00pm in California on the west coast. Based on the information given, which direction does Earth rotate on its axis?

    Ⓐ Clockwise as viewed from above the north pole

    Ⓑ Counterclockwise as viewed from above the north pole

    Ⓒ Toward the Sun

    Ⓓ The direction varies depending on the season

4. A boy is outside in the winter and notices that he begins shivering when he gets cold. A girl is outside during the summer and begins sweating when she gets hot. Why do the children's bodies react this way?

    Ⓐ The children's bodies are attempting to regulate their temperature

    Ⓑ The children's bodies are trying to fight off disease

    Ⓒ The children's bodies are reacting to the amount of sunlight or shade

    Ⓓ The children are having an allergic reaction to something in the air

5. How does the tilt of Earth's axis cause seasons?

    Ⓐ A hemisphere experiences winter when that half of Earth is tilted away from the Sun. It experiences summer when that half of Earth is tilted towards the Sun

    Ⓑ A hemisphere experiences spring when that half of Earth is tilted away from the Sun. It experiences autumn when that half of Earth is tilted towards the Sun

    Ⓒ A hemisphere experiences summer when that half of Earth is tilted away from the Sun. It experiences winter when that half of Earth is tilted towards the Sun

    Ⓓ A hemisphere experiences autumn when that half of Earth is tilted away from the Sun. It experiences spring when that half of Earth is tilted towards the Sun

> **Power Fruit**
> All natural fruit juice that gives you energy all day long
> 35 mg of caffeine
> 50% daily value of Vitamin E
> 100% daily value of Vitamin C

6. The advertisement above shows the nutrition information for the new juice, "Power Fruit". Which conclusion can be made about Power Fruit?

    Ⓐ Power Fruit contains the daily value of caffeine

    Ⓑ Power Fruit provides all the vitamin C you need each day

    Ⓒ Power Fruit has 100% daily value of vitamin A

    Ⓓ Power Fruit does not contain iron

7. Which of the following sources of fresh water is unavailable for human use?

    Ⓐ Rivers

    Ⓑ Estuaries

    Ⓒ Aquifers

    Ⓓ Glaciers

8. How are igneous rocks formed?

    Ⓐ Years of sediment are laid down on top of each other and forced together

    Ⓑ Acid rain caused by pollution creates holes in metamorphic rocks

    Ⓒ Dust and pebbles are pressed together underground from Earth's heat and pressure

    Ⓓ Magma from a volcanic eruption cools and hardens

9. Jim and John are working on their science fair project when they accidently break a beaker. What should the boys do?

    Ⓐ Tell their teacher immediately

    Ⓑ Clean up the broken glass themselves

    Ⓒ Move away from the broken glass and continue working

    Ⓓ Hide the broken glass so they don't get in trouble

10. Why do balloons filled with helium float while balloons filled with air do not float?

Ⓐ Balloons filled with air are larger than balloons filled with helium, which makes them heavier preventing them from floating

Ⓑ Helium is less dense than air, which allows balloons filled with helium to float

Ⓒ Helium balloons travel on higher air currents and balloons filled with air travel on lower air currents

Ⓓ Air causes balloons to generate static electricity so the balloon will be attracted to the ground

11. Which of the following is the most likely food source for a carnivore?

Ⓐ A plant

Ⓑ The Sun

Ⓒ An animal

Ⓓ A dead tree

12. Why are plants considered producers?

Ⓐ They make their own food

Ⓑ They soak up water from the ground

Ⓒ Their leaves can be large or small

Ⓓ They produce pollen, which is a food source for many insects and birds

13. How should students determine the volume of fluid in a graduated cylinder?

Ⓐ Read the volume at the bottom of the meniscus

Ⓑ Read the volume at the highest point the fluid reaches

Ⓒ Read the volume at the center, between the meniscus and the highest point of the fluid

Ⓓ Read the volume at the highest point then round to the nearest tens

- 20 -

14. A student is conducting an experiment using a ball that is attached to the end of a string on a pendulum. The student pulls the ball back so that it is at an angle to its resting position. As the student releases the ball, it swings forward and backward. The student measures the time it takes the ball to make one complete period. A period is defined as the time it takes the ball to swing forward and back again to its starting position. This is repeated using different string lengths.

The student formed the following hypothesis: *Lengthening the string of the pendulum increases the time it takes the ball to make one complete period.*

What correction would you have the student make to the hypothesis?

   Ⓐ Turn it into an "if/then" statement

   Ⓑ Add the word "will" in the middle after the word "pendulum"

   Ⓒ Switch the order of the sentence so that the phrase about the period comes first, and the phrase about the string's length is last

   Ⓓ No corrections are needed

15. When should instructions for a laboratory experiment be read?

   Ⓐ Instructions only need to be read if the teacher does not explain the steps of the lab well

   Ⓑ The instructions should be read if the students get confused or are not sure of the steps in the lab

   Ⓒ Instructions should be read thoroughly before beginning the lab

   Ⓓ The instructions do not need to be read, they are only a suggestion for how to complete the lab

16. A ball is thrown and the distance it traveled is measured. Which data set corresponds to the graph below?

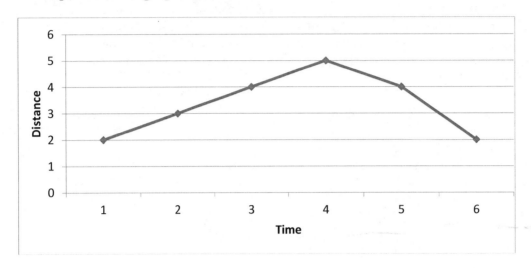

Ⓐ

Time	Distance
1	2
2	4
3	6
4	8
5	9

Ⓒ

Time	Distance
2	0
4	1
6	3
8	5
9	7

Ⓑ

Time	Distance
1	2
3	4
5	6
7	8
9	9

Ⓓ

Time	Distance
1	2
2	3
3	4
4	5
5	4
6	2

17. The data below was collected by repeating the same experiment four different times. What conclusion can be drawn based on the data shown?

Bicycle Obstacle Race

Student	Trial 1	Trial 2	Trial 3	Trial 4
Kayla	57.6 s	37.6 s	37.3 s	36.2 s
Carson	64.0 s	32.6 s	31.2 s	28.4 s
Jeremy	59.2 s	31.0 s	28.8 s	27.9 s
Rachel	61.3 s	42.6 s	39.5 s	39.0 s

Ⓐ The data was accurate in all four trials

Ⓑ The data in trials 2 through 4 is probably inaccurate

Ⓒ An error occurred in trial 1 that gave inaccurate data

Ⓓ The times in trial 4 are fastest because the students were tired

18. The first microscope was developed by Hans and Zacharias Janssen and allowed scientists to

Ⓐ See organisms too small to be seen with the naked eye

Ⓑ Count the number of organisms in the universe

Ⓒ Determine the causes of all human illness

Ⓓ Study why some females are taller than others

19. Electrical cords, such as the cords of a television or the cord on a toaster, are covered with rubber or plastic. What would you expect to happen if a portion of the rubber covering were missing when you tried to plug the cord in?

Ⓐ The appliance would not work after it was plugged in

Ⓑ The person plugging the appliance in would feel an electric shock

Ⓒ The appliance being plugged in would work, but all other appliances in the home would stop working

Ⓓ The cover does not matter, all appliances would work normally

20. Which of the statements below explains why a boy can run fast on the beach, but is much slower in water?

Ⓐ The boy is afraid of sharks and slows down when he enters the water

Ⓑ The boy cannot swim and stops running to avoid drowning

Ⓒ Water is thicker than air, which creates more resistance and slows the boy down

Ⓓ The force of the waves causes the boy to float, which prevents him from running

21. Place your answer on the provided griddable answer sheet.
In order to produce a constant supply of energy, solar panels require constant exposure to what? *Light Energy or Sun* (Sun) *provid energy*

22. Which statement accurately describes a state of matter?

Ⓐ Solids take the shape of their container

Ⓑ Gases maintain a fixed shape

Ⓒ Liquids will expand to fill the volume of a container

Ⓓ Gases expand to fill an entire space

23. Based on the weather forecast, what can a farmer expect to happen to his bird bath overnight?

10pm	11pm	12am	1am	2am	3am	4am	5am
34°C	25°C	11°C	2°C	-4 °C	-12 °C	-18°C	-18°C

Ⓐ Freeze

Ⓑ Evaporate

Ⓒ Melt

Ⓓ Sublime

24. The boiling point of water is 100°C. Adding salt raises the boiling point. What is the result of adding salt to water when cooking pasta?

Ⓐ The pasta cooks more slowly

Ⓑ The pasta will not stick together

Ⓒ The water will boil more quickly

Ⓓ The pasta will cook in hotter water

25. A man accidentally drops his wallet in a swimming pool. He can see his wallet at the bottom of the pool. He jumps in to retrieve it, but the wallet is not where it appeared to be. What is the reason for the optical illusion?

Ⓐ The reflection of sunlight off of the water disrupted his view

Ⓑ Light is refracted as it enters the water changing the wallet's apparent location

Ⓒ The current at the bottom of the pool caused the wallet to move

Ⓓ The heat from the Sun has impaired the man's vision

26. Two students spent several hours testing how well different running shoes supported athletes' feet. All of the following allow the students to effectively communicate the results of their experiment except

Ⓐ Create an advertisement that tells only the positive results of the shoes

Ⓑ Design a side by side comparison with graphs and conclusions that reveals all of the results of the experiment

Ⓒ Develop an oral report that presents their results

Ⓓ Write a paper that summarizes their experiment and results

27. The observations outlined below were made about a pot of water over a campfire. What is the most likely explanation for these observations?

- The pot was half full of water
- The pot hung over the campfire for 15 minutes
- The water began boiling after 7 minutes
- A white vapor was observed over the pot
- After 15 minutes, the pot was one quarter of the way full

Ⓐ Some of the water disappeared

Ⓑ The water changes from a gas to a liquid

Ⓒ Some of the water changed from a liquid to a gas, which was the vapor observed

Ⓓ The pot was never half full, someone measured incorrectly

28. A ball is resting on the front end of a boat. The boat is moving straight forwards toward a dock. When the front of the boat hits the dock, how will the ball's motion change?

Ⓐ The ball will remain at rest

Ⓑ The ball will move backwards

Ⓒ The ball will move forwards

Ⓓ The ball will move sideways

29. Which statement describes how fossil fuels are made?

Ⓐ Oil from Earth's core slowly rises to the Earth's surface and forms ponds

Ⓑ Lava within some volcanoes becomes so hot that is transforms into fossil fuels

Ⓒ Dead and decomposing organisms, exposed to extreme heat and pressure, transform into fossil fuels

Ⓓ When mountains form on top of coal, the pressure liquefies the coal creating fossil fuels

30. The Sahara desert receives about 3.6 inches of precipitation per year. Antarctica is also a desert receiving between 3 to 8 inches of precipitation per year. What makes an area a desert?

Ⓐ The temperature

Ⓑ The amount of animal life

Ⓒ The number of people living in the region

Ⓓ The yearly precipitation

31. What question are the students most likely testing with the experiment outlined below?

Seed type: Pansy Water: ½ gallon daily Soil: Bob's soil Daylight: 3 hours per day Flower color: Blue	Seed type: Pansy Water: ½ gallon daily Soil: Texas dirt Daylight: 3 hours per day Flower color: Purple	Seed type: Pansy Water: ½ gallon daily Soil: Grow Up Dirt Daylight: 3 hours per day Flower color: red

Ⓐ Does the amount of water affect how tall a flower will grow?

Ⓑ Does the type of soil affect the color of a flower?

Ⓒ What color of flower do bees prefer?

Ⓓ Is three hours of daylight enough for flowers to grow?

32. A prairie ecosystem is described below. Which organisms from the ecosystem are carnivores?

Grass is eaten by grasshoppers, rabbits, and crickets
Corn is eaten by squirrels and beetles
Grasshoppers, beetles, and crickets are all eaten by birds
Squirrels, birds, and rabbits are all eaten by both foxes and coyotes

Ⓐ Corn and grass

Ⓑ Grasshoppers and crickets

Ⓒ Beetles and birds

Ⓓ Foxes and coyotes

33. In a food chain, where does energy go after the secondary consumer dies?

Ⓐ Back to the Sun

Ⓑ To the producers

Ⓒ Into air, becomes wind

Ⓓ To decomposers

34. Every year thousands of square miles of trees are cut down to make paper products. Which of the following is not a result of cutting down trees?

Ⓐ Animals experience a loss of habitat

Ⓑ There is a decrease in the amount of oxygen available

Ⓒ There is a decrease in the amount of food available to herbivores and omnivores

Ⓓ There is a decrease in the amount of CO_2 in the atmosphere

35. According to the data below, what can be determined about Saturn?

Planet	Length of Year	Length of Day
Venus	224.7 days	116.75 days
Earth	365 days	24 hours
Saturn	10,759 days	10 hours 32 minutes
Neptune	164.79 years	16.11 hours

Ⓐ Saturn takes the least amount of time to rotate on its axis.

Ⓑ Saturn is the furthest planet from the Sun.

Ⓒ The further a planet is from the Sun, the shorter its day will be.

Ⓓ The larger a planet is, the longer its day will be.

- 27 -

36. A dog is an omnivore. What would you expect a dog's diet to consist of?

Ⓐ Meat

Ⓑ Vegetables

Ⓒ Both meat and vegetables

Ⓓ Neither meat nor vegetables

37. The following represents a simple food chain. What trophic level contains the greatest amount of energy?

Tree → Caterpillar → Frog → Snake → Hawk → Worm

Ⓐ Tree

Ⓑ Caterpillar

Ⓒ Hawk

Ⓓ Worm

38. How are organisms, such as snakes, cacti, and coyotes, able to survive in harsh desert conditions?

Ⓐ Over thousands of years these organisms have developed adaptations to survive in arid climates

Ⓑ These organisms migrate out of the desert during the summer months, only living in the desert for a portion of the year

Ⓒ Snakes, cacti, and coyotes work together to find sources of food and water

Ⓓ Snakes, cacti, and coyotes are all aquatic species that live in ponds and rivers during the hot day

X 39. A student is building a model of the Solar System using produce from the local supermarket. What order should she put the objects in to correctly represent the Solar System?

Object in Solar System	Model	Object in Solar System	Model
Mars	Raspberry	Uranus	tomato
Saturn	Grapefruit	Mercury	raisin
The Sun	Watermelon	Venus	grape
Jupiter	Lettuce	Asteroid Belt	sunflower seeds
Earth	Cherry	Neptune	orange

Ⓐ Watermelon-raisin-grape-cherry-raspberry-tomato-orange-lettuce-grapefruit-seeds

Ⓑ Watermelon-raisin-grape-cherry-raspberry-seeds-lettuce-grapefruit-tomato-orange

Ⓒ Watermelon-lettuce-grapefruit-tomato-orange-cherry-grape-raspberry-raisin-seeds

Ⓓ Watermelon-grape-raisin-cherry-seeds-raspberry-lettuce-grapefruti-orange-tomato

40. Why is it important to form a hypothesis before performing an experiment?

Ⓐ The experimenter will not have enough time to create a hypothesis after beginning the experiment

Ⓑ Developing a hypothesis ensures that the lab will be safe

Ⓒ The experiment will take too much time to complete if there is no hypothesis

Ⓓ The hypothesis tells what the experiment is going to be testing

41. A student is working on a science project and is going through each step of the scientific method. After the student conducts his or her first experiment and records the results of the experimental test, what should the student do next?

Ⓐ Communicate the results

Ⓑ Draw a conclusion

Ⓒ Repeat the experiment

Ⓓ Create a hypothesis

42. Which of the following is considered a non-renewable resource?

Ⓐ Glass

Ⓑ Wood

Ⓒ Cattle

Ⓓ Soil

- 29 -

43. How is force being applied to the box below?

BOX

Ⓐ The box is being pulled forward

Ⓑ The box is being pushed forward

Ⓒ Gravity is forcing the box to move forward

Ⓓ Friction is forcing the box to stop

44. What is the benefit of a kangaroo's large ears?

Ⓐ They improve the kangaroo's vision

Ⓑ Large ears help kangaroos taste their food

Ⓒ Large ears allow kangaroos to outrun predators

Ⓓ Large ears help kangaroos hear predators coming

- 30 -

Answers and Explanations

TEKS Standard §112.16(b)(4)(A)

1. B: Thermometers are used to measure temperature. Graduated cylinders are used to measure volume while a ruler is used to measure distance. Balances are used to measure mass.

TEKS Standard §112.16(b)(3) and (6)(D)

2. C: Wheel A is turning clockwise, which causes wheel B to turn counterclockwise. Wheel B then causes wheel C to turn clockwise. Wheel C in turn, turns wheel D in the counterclockwise direction. The question states that the wheels are in contact, and the number of intermediate wheels does not prevent the turning motion from being transferred all the way down the line.

TEKS Standard §112.16(b)(3) and (8)

3. B: The east coast, states such as Maine, New York, and New Hampshire are three hours ahead of states on the west coast such as California, Washington, and Oregon. Earth rotates west to east, and that is counterclockwise when viewed from above the North Pole.

TEKS Standard §112.16(b)(3) and (10)

4. A: The human body works best within a certain temperature range, around 98.6°F. When the body gets too cold or too hot it cannot function properly. The boy who is outside in the winter is cold. His body temperature is dropping below 98.6°F. His muscles start to contract causing him to shiver in order to generate heat. The girl is outside in the summer, and begins sweating to reduce her body temperature from rising too far above 98.6°F. In both cases, the children's bodies are trying to keep the temperature close to 98.6°F.

TEKS Standard §112.16(b)(8)

5. A: Heat on Earth is generated by the Sun. The more direct sunlight an area on Earth receives from the Sun, the warmer it will be. When the Northern hemisphere is tilted away from the Sun, all of the countries in the Northern hemisphere experience winter. At that same time, the Southern hemisphere experiences summer. The same is true when the Southern hemisphere experiences winter; the Northern hemisphere experiences summer.

TEKS Standard §112.16(b)(3)(B)

6. B: The advertisement states that Power Fruit contains 100% of the daily value of vitamin C, which means that it meets the amount of vitamin C a person needs each day. The ad also states that Power Fruit contains 35 mg of caffeine, but there is no indication of what the daily value of caffeine is. There is no mention of vitamin A or iron anywhere in the advertisement.

TEKS Standard §112.16(b)(3)

7. D: Glaciers and ice caps are fresh water unavailable for human use as they are frozen. The hydrologic cycle refers to all the water on planet Earth. Some water is in forms that humans do not tend to use, such as oceans (too salty and expensive to desalinate) and glaciers. Water suitable for drinking can be found as surface water and in ground water, which is

- 31 -

obtained through wells. Answers A, Rivers, B, Estuaries, and C, Aquifers, are all examples of surface water that are available to humans.

TEKS Standard §112.16(b)(7)

8. D: Igneous rocks are formed when magma in Earth erupts through cracks in the crust where it cools creating a hard structure with many air pockets or holes.

TEKS Standard §112.16(b)(1)(A)

9. A: Anytime there is an accident in the lab, the first step is always to tell the teacher. Even if a student or students were doing something that they should not have been doing, such as horse playing in the lab, the teacher's first priority is still to make sure the students are safe. Telling the teacher will allow him or her to respond appropriately to the situation and make sure that all of the students remain safe.

TEKS Standard §112.16(b)(5)(A)

10. B: The air we breathe is composed of many types of molecules, and is quite heavy compared to helium. The reason helium balloons float is because helium is less dense than the surrounding air. Objects that are less dense will float in objects that are more dense, as a helium balloon does when surrounded by air.

TEKS Standard §112.16(b)(9)

11. C: The prefix *carni-* means flesh, so carnivores are flesh eaters. Their diet consists of meats. The only answer choice that is a meat is an animal.

TEKS Standard §112.16(b)(9)

12. A: Plants are considered producers because they are able to absorb light energy from the Sun and convert it into food through the process of photosynthesis. In other words, plants are producers because they produce their own food from sunlight.

TEKS Standard §112.16(b)(2)(C) and (4)(A)

13. A: The volume of a graduated cylinder should be read at the bottom of the meniscus.

TEKS Standard §112.16(b)(2)(F)

14. A: Turn it into an "if/then" statement. A formalized hypothesis written in the form of an if/then statement can then be tested. A statement may make a prediction or imply a cause/effect relationship, but that does not necessarily make it a good hypothesis. In this example, having the student rewrite the statement in the form of an if/then statement could read: If the length of the string of the pendulum is varied, then the time it takes the ball to make one complete period changes. This hypothesis is testable, doesn't simply make a prediction, nor does it give a conclusion. The validity of the hypothesis can then be supported or disproved by experimentation and observation.

TEKS Standard §112.16(b)(1)(A)

15. C: Laboratory instructions not only contain steps to the procedure, but also often contain important safety information. The instructions should always be read before beginning the lab. Any questions should be addressed by the instructor before starting an experiment.

TEKS Standard §112.16(b)(2)(D) and (2)(G)

16. D: The graph represents a set of data. The line graph increases in distance from 1 second to 4 seconds and then begins decreasing. The only data set that shows distance increasing and then decreasing is set D.

TEKS Standard §112.16(b)(2)(E)

17. C: The data is relatively consistent with the exception of trial 1. When an experiment is repeated using the same process multiple times, the data from each trial should be very similar or the same. The results of trial 1 indicate that an error may have occurred in the procedure yielding inaccurate results.

TEKS Standard §112.16(b)(3)(D)

18. A: The microscope was discovered when a series of lenses were placed in a specific order magnifying objects that were too small to see otherwise. The development of the microscope also led to discoveries such as the cell, bacteria, and fungi.

TEKS Standard §112.16(b)(6)

19. B: The purpose of the rubber coating on the outside of electrical cords is to contain the electric current in the metal wire. When part of the rubber coating is missing, the electric current can leave the wire and cause an electric shock to the person plugging in the wire.

TEKS Standard §112.16(b)(5)(A)

20. C: Water is denser than air and creates more resistance on the boy running. Air is thin and this allows the boy to run fast on the beach.

TEKS Standard §112.16(b)(7)(C)

21. Sun. The word *solar* refers to the sun. Solar panels are large panels that absorb energy from the sun and convert it into other types of energy, such as electrical energy, that can be used to power anything from a car to a toaster. If there is no sun, such as at night, the panels do not take in any solar energy to convert to electricity. The amount of energy each solar panel can produce depends on the amount of sunlight it is exposed to.

TEKS Standard §112.16(b)(5)(A)

22. D: The molecules that make up gases are far apart and move about very quickly. Because they have a weak attraction to each other, they expand to take up as much space as possible.

TEKS Standard §112.16(b)(5)(B)

23. A: The weather forecast shows that a cold front will be arriving in the area causing the temperature to drop from 34°C to -18°C. The freezing point of water is 0°C, which means that the water in the birdbath will freeze overnight after the cold front arrives.

TEKS Standard §112.16(b)(5)(B)

24. D: Adding salt to water causes the boiling point of water to rise. The water has to reach a temperature beyond 100°C in order to boil, so the water will be hotter when the pasta cooks. It is a common misconception that because the salt water is boiling at a higher temperature, the pasta will cook faster. The increase in temperature is too slight to make a significant difference in cooking time.

TEKS Standard §112.16(b)(6)(C)

25. B: Light travels faster in air than it can in water. Water molecules are closer together than air particles are, which causes the light to slow down and bend as it enters the water. The bending of light is called refraction and creates the illusion of the wallet being next to where it actually is.

TEKS Standard §112.16(b)(2)(F)

26. A: The purpose of a scientific experiment is to collect as much reliable data as possible about a specific hypothesis. Scientists can use the results from other experiments to help them determine what hypothesis to test next. Creating an advertisement that tells only the positive aspects of the running shoes would omit any negative aspects of the shoes that may be relevant. The results would not be reliable because they would be incomplete.

TEKS Standard §112.16(b)(5)

27. C: Water boils at 100°C. As the pot of water heats up over the campfire, it begins to boil causing the liquid water to turn into water vapor, a gas. The vapor the campers observed over the boiling pot of water was water vapor. As the water continues to boil, more of the liquid turns into gas resulting in a decrease in the volume of water in the pot.

TEKS Standard §112.16(b)(6)

28. C: The ball will move forwards. The ball is moving forward with the boat. When the front of the boat hits the dock, the ball's motion does not change. It continues to move forward because the force acting to stop the boat is not acting upon the ball. The forward motion of the boat is halted by the dock. The forward motion of the ball is not stopped. Since the ball is round there is little friction to provide an equal and opposite reaction to the forward motion.

TEKS Standard §112.16(b)(7)(A)

29. C: Organisms that lived millions of years ago have been covered up by many layers of earth. The temperature and pressure increases transforming the dead organisms into fossil fuels that can be obtained and used for energy.

TEKS Standard §112.16(b)(8)

30. D: A desert is classified by the average amount of precipitation the region receives on a yearly basis. The temperature is irrelevant, as there are both hot and cold deserts. Due to the dry conditions, only organisms designed to withstand the arid conditions can survive in these areas.

TEKS Standard §112.16(b)(2)(A) and (3)

31. B: In order to determine the question being tested, you must look at the data given. Answer choice A asks about how tall a flower will grow, but the height of the flowers is not given, so this cannot be what was tested. Answer choice C asks about bees, which are also not referenced anywhere in the experiment. Answer choice D asks about the amount of daylight required for the flowers to grow. All three flowers were given the same amount of daylight- three hours, so this cannot be what is tested. The only change between each of the tests is the type of dirt used, which affected the flower color.

TEKS Standard §112.16(b)(9)(A)

32. D: Carnivores eat meat only. In the ecosystem described, both coyotes and foxes are carnivores eating squirrels, birds, and rabbits.

TEKS Standard §112.16(b)(9)(B)

33. D: After a secondary consumer dies, such as a wolf, its body is partially consumed by decomposers, such as bacteria and fungi. Bacteria and fungi live in soil and digest body tissues of dead organisms converting them into basic nutrients that plants need to grow. Therefore, after secondary consumers die, their energy is consumed by decomposers, who make nutrients available in the soil for producers to use. *Do not confuse nutrients in the soil with energy that producers get from the Sun to make their own food.*

TEKS Standard §112.16(b)(9)(D)

34. D: Trees absorb and use carbon dioxide to produce their own food. Humans breathe in oxygen and breathe out carbon dioxide. To a human, too much carbon dioxide is toxic and can cause serious problems. Plants use carbon dioxide and release oxygen as waste. This allows what is toxic to humans, carbon dioxide, to be used and transformed into breathable oxygen. A decrease in the number of trees decreases the amount of plants taking in carbon dioxide, causing the carbon dioxide levels in the atmosphere to rise.

TEKS Standard §112.16(b)(8)(C)

35. A: When a planet rotates on its axis it creates day and night. The side of the planet that faces away from the Sun is in night. When that side rotates around to face the Sun, it is in day. The data indicates that Saturn takes the least amount of time to rotate on its axis, which indicates that is has the shortest day at only 10 hours and 32 minutes.

TEKS Standard §112.16(b)(9)

36. C: The prefix *omni-*means all, so an omnivore eats all types of food. Omnivores, such as dogs and many humans, eat a variety of plants and meats to achieve a balanced diet.

TEKS Standard §112.16(b)(9)

37. A: In the food chain of Tree → Caterpillar → Frog → Snake → Hawk → Worm, the tree is at the trophic level with the greatest amount of energy. Trophic level refers to the position of an organism in a food chain. Energy is lost according to the laws of thermodynamics as one moves up the food chain because it is converted to heat when consumers consume. Primary producers, such as autotrophs, are organisms who are at the base and capture solar energy. Primary consumers are herbivores that feed on the producers. Secondary consumers consume primary consumers and so on. Decomposers get their energy from the consumption of dead plants and animals.

TEKS Standard §112.16(b)(10)(A)

38. A: Many organisms, especially organisms that live in harsh conditions such as deserts or frozen icy areas, have developed specific adaptations that allow them to survive. For example, cacti are able to expand to store large amounts of water, coyotes absorb some water from their food, and snakes can escape the heat by hiding within rocks.

TEKS Standard §112.16(b)(8)

39. B: This question is really asking you to determine the correct order of the major bodies in the Solar System. The correct order is: Sun (watermelon), Mercury (raisin), Venus (grape), Earth (cherry), Mars (raspberry), asteroid belt (seeds), Jupiter (lettuce), Saturn (grapefruit), Uranus (tomato), Neptune (orange).

TEKS Standard §112.16(b)(2)(A)

40. D: A hypothesis predicts what the experimenter thinks is going to happen and why. It is based on prior knowledge and research. An experiment is designed to test the hypothesis. Without a hypothesis, an experiment cannot be designed or performed.

TEKS Standard §112.16(b)(2)(E)

41. C: Repeating the experiment validates data. Each separate experiment is called a repetition. Results of experiments or tests should be able to be replicated. Similar data gathered from many experiments can also be used to quantify the validity of the hypothesis. Repeating the experiments allows the student to observe variation in the results. Variation in data can be caused by a variety of errors or may be disproving the hypothesis. Answer D, Create a hypothesis, comes before experiments. Answers A, Communicate the results, and B, Draw a conclusion, occur after testing.

TEKS Standard §112.16(b)(7)

42. A: Glass is considered a non-renewable resource. Glass is manufactured and can be recycled, but is considered a non-renewable resource. Answer B, Wood, is considered a renewable resource because with proper management, an equilibrium can be reached between harvesting trees and planting new ones. Cattle, Answer C, are managed in herds and a balance can be achieved between those consumed and those born. Answer D, Soil, is the result of long-term erosion and includes organic matter and minerals needed by plants. Soil found naturally in the environment is renewed. Crops can be rotated to help maintain a healthy soil composition for farming.

TEKS Standard §112.16(b)(6)

43. A: The picture shows an arrow in front of the box pulling the box forward. If the box were being pushed, the arrow would be behind the box pushing it forward. Gravity pulls downward, not forward.

TEKS Standard §112.16(b)(10)(A)

44. D: Kangaroos live in a dry, wide-open environment where there is little coverage from predators. It is important for kangaroos to be able to hear predators coming from a far distance so they can escape. Their large ears help them to hear subtle sounds of potential predators from far away.

Practice Test

100'1.   44/44

1. **A prairie ecosystem is described below. Farmers treat fields surrounding the prairie with pesticides that kill part of the beetle population. What effect would the pesticides have on the rest of the ecosystem?**

Grass is eaten by grasshoppers, rabbits, and crickets
Corn is eaten by squirrels and beetles
Grasshoppers, beetles, and crickets are all eaten by birds
Squirrels, birds, and rabbits are all eaten by both foxes and coyotes

Ⓐ There would be a decrease in the cricket population.

Ⓑ There would be an increase in the population of birds.

Ⓒ The population of rabbits would decrease.

Ⓓ The population of foxes would increase.

2. **Which organisms from the ecosystem described above are herbivores?**

Ⓐ Corn and grass

Ⓑ Grasshoppers and crickets

Ⓒ Beetles and birds

Ⓓ Foxes and coyotes

3. **Which statement correctly describes the relationship between plants and animals?**

Ⓐ Animals breathe in oxygen and plants release oxygen.

Ⓑ Animals breathe in carbon dioxide while plants release carbon dioxide.

Ⓒ Animals breathe in carbon dioxide while plants breathe out carbon dioxide.

Ⓓ Animals get oxygen from plants by eating the plants.

4. Which picture best represents Earth's position on its axis?

 Ⓐ

 Ⓑ

 Ⓒ

 Ⓓ

5. What should be included in a hypothesis?

Ⓐ A hypothesis should tell what you think is going to happen and why.

Ⓑ A hypothesis should state what the results of similar experiments were.

Ⓒ A hypothesis should summarize the results of an experiment.

Ⓓ A hypothesis should compare the control to the variable.

6. What causes high and low tide?

Ⓐ The Earth's rotation

Ⓑ The Moon's gravity

Ⓒ The wind currents

Ⓓ The change in water temperature

7. Earth rotates on its axis every 24 hours and revolves around the Sun every 365 earth days. Mars revolves around the Sun every 687 earth days. What does a period 687 earth days represent in terms of Mars time?

Ⓐ One Martian day

Ⓑ One Martian year

Ⓒ One Martian season

Ⓓ One Martian month

8. What does a food chain show?

   Ⓐ The flow of energy between organisms

   Ⓑ Very type of species living in a habitat

   Ⓒ The population of each species in a habitat

   Ⓓ The number of offspring a species will produce in a year

9. Lions live in savannah and grassland regions where there are tall dry grasses. Lions must sneak up and stalk their prey. What is the most likely reason for a lion's sand colored coat?

   Ⓐ It allows lions to hide within the grass

   Ⓑ The light color of their coat reflects heat from the Sun

   Ⓒ A lion's coloring helps it attract mates

   Ⓓ It allows them to run faster than their prey

10. In which of the following scenarios is Mario not applying work to a book?

   Ⓐ Mario moves a book from the floor to the top shelf of a bookcase

   Ⓑ Mario lets go of a book that he is holding so that it falls to the floor

   Ⓒ Mario pushes a box of books across the room

   Ⓓ Mario balances a book on his head and walks across the room

11. Wind farms are one source of alternative energy, energy that can be used in place of fossil fuels. The amount of energy a wind farm produces is determined by

   Ⓐ Sunlight

   Ⓑ Season

   Ⓒ Wind

   Ⓓ Rainfall

12. A carnivore would eat all of the following except

   Ⓐ Rabbits

   Ⓑ Acorns

   Ⓒ Fish

   Ⓓ Deer

13. What instrument should be used to measure how fast a boy can run 100 meters?

Ⓐ Beaker

Ⓑ Meterstick

Ⓒ Stopwatch

Ⓓ Thermometer

14. Students have just completed a lab. What can they do to be sure that their results are reliable?

Ⓐ Repeat the lab again

Ⓑ Compare their data to data collected in similar experiments

Ⓒ Measure all of their results twice with two different rulers

Ⓓ Make sure that their results confirm that their hypothesis was correct

15. What would be the best material to make a cooking pot out of?

Ⓐ Rubber

Ⓑ Copper

Ⓒ Plastic

Ⓑ Cement

16. Flowers, trees, and shrubs are all examples of what?

Ⓐ Carnivores

Ⓑ Herbivores

Ⓒ Producers

Ⓓ Predators

17. Why can a person see their reflection in a mirror?

Ⓐ Light is scattered when it hits a mirror producing a backward image

Ⓑ Light is reflected off of the mirror back towards the person standing in front of it

Ⓒ Light bends as it passes through the mirror creating an optical illusion

Ⓓ Light is refracted, which produces a mirror image behind the glass

18. A tropical flower is planted in a local garden. The garden is watered 2 to 3 times per week during all seasons. After only a few months the tropical plant begins to droop and turn brown. How did environmental change most likely affect the tropical plant?

(A) Being watered 2 to 3 times per week was not enough to sustain a tropical plant

(B) The new environment was too hot and burned the plant

(C) Insects attacked the plant causing it to wilt

(D) The new soil lacked the nutrients necessary to maintain the plant's health

19. Place your answer on the provided griddable answer sheet. How many planets are in Earth's solar system?   8 planets

20. What type of satellite is Pluto?

(A) Planet

(B) Comet

(C) Dwarf planet

(D) Asteroid

21. Algae are part of many food chains. How do algae produce energy?

algae   fish   seal   shark

(A) They hunt fish for food

(B) Algae undergo photosynthesis

(C) They decompose dead or dying organisms

(D) They consume fossil fuel from beneath Earth's surface

- 41 -

22. Four windows are washed with different cleaners. The same paper towel is used on each. The squares below show each window before being cleaned. What is the variable in the experiment?

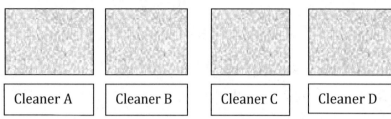

| Cleaner A | Cleaner B | Cleaner C | Cleaner D |

Ⓐ The amount of sunlight coming through the windows

Ⓑ The type of window cleaner used

Ⓒ The amount of dirt on each window

Ⓓ The type of paper towel used

23. Why is it more difficult to push a shopping cart full of groceries than an empty shopping cart?

Ⓐ The full cart has less mass than the empty cart

Ⓑ The full cart has a greater mass than the empty cart

Ⓒ The full cart has less friction than the empty cart

Ⓓ The empty cart is not pulled down by gravity

24. Use the information in the table to determine what would happen to the mass and weight of a human if he or she were on Neptune.

Mass	Mass is the amount of matter there is. Mass only changes when matter is added or removed.
Weight	Weight is how much gravity pulls downward on an object. The more gravity there is, the more an object weighs.
Gravity on Earth: 9.8 m/s²	Gravity on Neptune: 11.15 m/s²

Ⓐ A person's mass and weight would increase on Neptune

Ⓑ A person's mass and weight would decrease on Neptune

Ⓒ A person's mass would increase, but weight would be unchanged

Ⓓ A person's mass would be unchanged, but weight would increase

25. Look at the two images of a spring shown below. The first is a spring before it has been stretched by a force. The second is the same spring after it has been stretched by a force. Use your ruler to determine how far the force caused the spring to stretch?

Before Force

After force

Ⓐ 0.2 cm

Ⓑ 0.5 cm

Ⓒ 1.0 cm

Ⓓ 1.5 cm

26. How are the size of a dog and the pitch of its bark related?

Breed	Height from ground to back	Pitch of Bark
Chihuahua	20 cm	17 Hz
Cocker Spaniel	45 cm	14 Hz
Labrador	63 cm	12 Hz
Dalmatian	78 cm	11 Hz
Great Dane	114 cm	8 Hz

Ⓐ The smaller breeds have a lower pitch bark than the larger breeds

Ⓑ The size of the dog has no relationship to the pitch of the bark

Ⓒ The larger breeds have a lower pitch bark than the smaller breeds

Ⓓ The smallest breed and largest breed have the highest pitch barks

27. How are we able to see the Moon on a dark night?

Ⓐ The Moon reflects light from the Sun, which illuminates the Moon

Ⓑ The Moon generates energy that makes it glow

Ⓒ The Moon reflects heat from the Sun that causes it to glow

Ⓓ The Moon's surface is covered in active volcanoes that glow when they erupt

28. In the diagram shown below, four wheels are in contact such that each wheel turns the opposite direction from the wheels it is touching. Wheel A is being turned clockwise by a force as shown. What direction is wheel C turning?

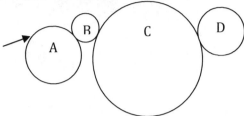

    Ⓐ Wheel C does not turn at all because it is too much larger than wheel B

    Ⓑ Wheel C does not turn at all because it is not touching wheel B

    Ⓒ Wheel C turns counterclockwise

    Ⓓ Wheel C turns clockwise

29. Water is stored underground, as well as in oceans and ice caps. Such underground storage reservoirs are called:

    Ⓐ Storage tanks

    Ⓑ Aquifers

    Ⓒ Evaporators

    Ⓓ Runoff

30. An ice cube tray is filled with water. The tray is placed in a freezer for 12 hours. The water freezes forming ice. The tray is removed from the freezer and left on a counter for 12 hours. What changes as the water becomes ice and then melts back into water?

    Ⓐ The amount of energy in the water

    Ⓑ The amount of water in the ice cube tray

    Ⓒ The number of water molecules

    Ⓓ The mass of the water molecules

31. Several people were asked to jump on a large trampoline, one at a time, to see who could jump the highest. The results were recorded in the data table below.

Person	Weight	Highest Jump
Sarah	59 kg	1.35 m
Mark	75 kg	1.81 m
Isaac	78 kg	1.93 m
Valerie	64 kg	1.47 m
Crystal	66 kg	1.57 m

Based on the data, what can be concluded about the relationship between weight and jumping height?

(A) The more a person weighs, the higher he or she could jump

(B) The less a person weighs, the higher he or she could jump

(C) A person's weight does not affect how high he or she was able to jump

(D) The taller the person is, the higher he or she could jump

32. Which statement describes how Earth's relationship to the Sun allows the polar ice caps to remain frozen?

(A) The equator receives the most direct sunlight while the poles receive the least amount of sunlight

(B) The Moon reflects the Sun's light away from the North and South Pole preventing them from heating up

(C) Wind currents constantly move air warmed by the Sun away from the North and South Pole and toward the equator

(D) The Sun does not shine on the North or South Pole so they never warm up

33. A Tsunami may be caused by:

(A) Earthquakes

(B) Volcanoes

(C) Landslides

(D) A, B, and C

34. **Which piece of safety equipment is designed to protect your eyes?**

Ⓐ Glasses

Ⓑ Goggles

Ⓒ Gloves

Ⓓ Eye wash

35. **How is force being applied to the box below?**

$\longrightarrow$ BOX

Ⓐ The box is being pulled forward

Ⓑ The box is being pushed forward

Ⓒ Gravity is forcing the box to move forward

Ⓓ Friction is forcing the box to stop

36. **Your teacher gives you a beaker of water and a beaker of vinegar. Both liquids are clear. What is the best way to distinguish between the two liquids?**

Ⓐ Take a small sip of each liquid, the vinegar will taste bad

Ⓑ Put your nose directly over each beaker and inhale deeply, the vinegar will smell bad

Ⓒ Add some baking soda to each beaker, the vinegar will react and form bubbles

Ⓓ Ask your teacher to label the beakers before handing them to you

37. **Which of the following does not represent a physical change?**

Ⓐ Salt dissolved in water

Ⓑ A spoiling apple

Ⓒ Sand dissolved in water

Ⓓ Pulverized rock

38. **Polar bears, seals and walrus' are all arctic animals that have a thick layer of blubber or fat beneath their skin. What purpose does this layer of blubber serve?**

Ⓐ Protects them from predators

Ⓑ Helps to preserve body heat

Ⓒ Aids in finding food

Ⓓ Prevents them from drowning in water

39. What does not need to be done after performing an experiment?

Ⓐ Wash hands

Ⓑ Brush hair

Ⓒ Clean up area

Ⓓ Complete the lab assignment

40. Why do some cacti have folds in their outer skin?

Ⓐ The folds can expand, allowing the cacti to absorb and store water when it rains

Ⓑ The folds help protect the cacti from predators

Ⓒ The folds allow them to absorb nutrients from the air

Ⓓ The folds provide support, allowing the cacti to grow tall

41. The factor most responsible for determining which season an area is experiencing is

Ⓐ Elevation

Ⓑ The position of the earth in its orbit around the sun

Ⓒ Latitude

Ⓓ Air masses

42. After a science laboratory exercise, some solutions remain unused and are left over. What should be done with these solutions?

Ⓐ Dispose of the solutions according to local disposal procedures

Ⓑ Empty the solutions into the sink and rinse with warm water and soap

Ⓒ Ensure the solutions are secured in closed containers and throw away

Ⓓ Store the solutions in a secured, dry place for later use

43. Compared to fresh water, the freezing point of sea water is

Ⓐ Higher

Ⓑ Lower

Ⓒ About the same

Ⓓ Sea water does not freeze

44. The formation of sedimentary rock includes all of the following processes except

Ⓐ Layering

Ⓑ Cementation

Ⓒ Compaction

Ⓓ Heat

Answers and Explanations

TEKS Standard §112.16(b)(9)(A)

1. A: In the ecosystem described, birds eat beetles, crickets, and grasshoppers. If a pesticide were to kill off part of the beetle population, birds would be forced to consume more crickets and grasshoppers to meet their energy needs. As a result, there would be a decrease in the cricket population.

TEKS Standard §112.16(b)(9)

2. B: Herbivores are organisms that eat producers (plants) only. In the ecosystem described, both grasshoppers and crickets are herbivores, eating corn and grass.

TEKS Standard §112.16(b)(9)(A)

3. A: Animals breathe in oxygen and breathe out carbon dioxide in a process called respiration. Plants use the carbon dioxide that animals exhale, in the process of photosynthesis, and convert it into oxygen.

TEKS Standard §112.16(b)(8)(C)

4. A: Earth sits on its axis at a tilt of 23.4°. Choice B would result in Earth rotating sideways and choice C is straight up and down. Choice D is not even physically possible.

TEKS Standard §112.16(b)(2)(B)

5. A: A hypothesis is an educated guess formulated by the experimenter based on prior experiments and research. A hypothesis includes what the experimenters think is going to happen and their reasoning.

TEKS Standard §112.16(b)(8)(B)

6. B: Tides are caused by the effect of the Moon's gravity and the Sun's gravity pulling on the ocean waters.

TEKS Standard §112.16(b)(8)(C)

7. B: A year is determined by the number of days it takes for a body to make one revolution around the Sun. So a Martian year would be the number of days it takes for Mars to orbit the Sun.

TEKS Standard §112.16(b)(9)

8. A: A food chain shows how energy flows from one consumer to another. The arrows point in the direction that energy moves. For example, if an arrow points from a flower to a bee, then the energy from the flower flows to the bee as the bee eats the nectar of the flower.

TEKS Standard §112.16(b)(10)(A)

9. A: Lions live in a wide open area where there are few large objects to hide behind. In order to get close enough to their prey to chase and attack it, they must be able to sneak up on it. Their coloration is similar to the color of the tall grasses where they live. This allows the lions to blend into their surroundings and get close to their prey.

TEKS Standard §112.16(b)(6)

10. B: When Mario lets go of the book, he is no longer exerting any force on it, so he cannot be doing work on it. In all the other examples, Mario is exerting a force on the book in the direction that it is moving. In Answer A, Mario moves a book from the floor to the top shelf. Mario lifted up vertically on the book, in the same direction that the book moved, so he was doing work. In Answer C, Mario pushes a box of books across the room. This is also an example of work being done because the box moved in the direction of the force Mario applied. In Answer D, Mario is indirectly applying a horizontal force to the book because of the friction between the book and his head, so he is exerting a force on the book in the direction he is moving.

TEKS Standard §112.16(b)(7)(C)

11. C: Wind farms harvest energy from wind to use in combination with or in place of fossil fuels. The biggest limiting factors for wind farms are the inconsistency and unpredictability of wind and the difficulties involved in storing the energy that has been harvested. Wind farms can only produce as much energy as they receive from wind.

TEKS Standard §112.16(b)(9)

12. B: Carnivores eat meat only. The only choice that is not meat is acorns, which are plant products.

TEKS Standard §112.16(b)(4)(A)

13. C: In this case, the term "how long" refers to the time it takes to do something, such as how long it takes a boy to run 100 meters. The instrument to measure time is a stopwatch.

TEKS Standard §112.16(b)(2)(E)

14. A: To be the more precise, the students could complete the lab again. In fact, all scientific laws have been developed by being tested over and over again through repetitive scientific experiment.

TEKS Standard §112.16(b)(5)(A)

15. B: A cooking pot must be able to conduct heat from the stove into the food being prepared. The only material that is a conductor from the choices given is copper.

TEKS Standard §112.16(b)(9)(B)

16. C: Flowers, trees, and shrubs are all plants, which are producers. Producers are able to make their own food using energy from the Sun in a process known as photosynthesis.

TEKS Standard §112.16(b)(6)(C)

17. B: A mirror is a reflective surface. The flat shiny surface reflects any incoming light allowing a person standing in front of the mirror to see their reflection.

TEKS Standard §112.16(b)(9)

18. A: Tropical environments typically receive rain 5 to 6 times per week, even if it is only a brief afternoon shower. In its new environment the tropical plant is not receiving enough water to survive.

TEKS Standard §112.16(b)(8)

19. There are eight planets in our solar system: **Mercury, Venus, Earth, Mars, Jupiter, Saturn, Uranus, and Neptune.**

TEKS Standard §112.16(b)(8)

20. C: Pluto was originally classified as a planet but in 2006, it was changed to a dwarf planet because of other similar type objects orbiting very close to it.

TEKS Standard §112.16(b)(9)

21. B: Algae are a type of plant that grows in water. Because algae are plants they are able to capture light from the Sun and transform it into energy during the process of photosynthesis.

TEKS Standard §112.16(b)(2)(A)

22. B: A variable is something that is changed in the experiment. It is being tested against other similar things. In this experiment, the variable is the type of window cleaner.

TEKS Standard §112.16(b)(6)

23. B: The empty shopping cart does not weigh very much and is easy to push. As groceries are added to the empty cart, the cart gains mass. By the time the shopping cart is full, it has more mass than it began with and requires more force to push it.

TEKS Standard §112.16(b)(3) and (5)

24. D: The table states that a person's mass remains the same, but weight will fluctuate with the force of gravity. It also states that the more gravity acting on an object, the more the object will weigh. Neptune has a greater gravitational force than Earth, so the person's weight would increase.

TEKS Standard §112.16(b)(4)(A)

25. B: The spring has a length of 1 cm before the force, and a length of 1.5 cm afterwards. The difference in lengths is 0.5 cm.

TEKS Standard §112.16(b)(2)(D)

26. C: The table shows that the largest dogs have the lowest pitch barks ranging from 8 to 12 hertz. The smaller dogs, such as the Chihuahua and spaniel, have higher pitch barks of 17 and 14 hertz.

TEKS Standard §112.16(b)(8)

27. A: The Moon does not emit any light of its own. However, the Moon does reflect light from the Sun. The phase of the Moon that we are able to see on Earth, such as full moon, crescent, or no moon, depends on where the Moon is positioned in relation to the Sun and Earth.

TEKS Standard §112.16(b)(3) and (6)(D)

28. D: Wheel A is turning clockwise, which causes wheel B to turn counterclockwise. Wheel B then causes wheel C to turn clockwise. The question states that the wheels are in contact, and while wheel C's size will cause it to rotate more slowly; it will not prevent it from turning.

TEKS Standard §112.16(b)(7)

29. B: An aquifer (a word derived from the Latin root *aqua*, meaning water) is any geologic formation containing ground water.

TEKS Standard §112.16(b)(5)(A)

30. A: When water changes from a liquid to a solid the amount of thermal energy is decreasing. The molecules move closer together, which creates the solid crystal structure of the ice. As the ice melts back into a liquid, thermal energy level increases, causing the molecules to spread out again.

TEKS Standard §112.16(b)(2)(D)

31. A: The table shows a clear correlation between mass and jump height. If you put the list of jumpers in order from highest mass to lowest mass, they will also be in order from highest jump height to lowest jump height. Choice D can be eliminated immediately because there is no information about any of the individuals' heights in the data table or in the question.

TEKS Standard §112.16(b)(8)

32. A: The equator receives the most direct sunlight while the North and South Pole receive the least amount of direct sunlight. In addition, the atmosphere helps to reflect some of the Sun's heat energy away from the poles. Finally, the reflectivity of the ice helps to deflect some of the heat away from the polar ice caps.

TEKS Standard §112.16(b)(8)

33. D: A tsunami, sometimes referred to as a tidal wave, is a large wave or series of waves caused by the displacement of a large volume of water. While the most common cause is an earthquake, large landslides (either falling into the sea or taking place under water) or explosive volcanic action may also result in a tsunami. Tsunamis take the appearance of very high, sustained tides, and may move water very far inland. Large storms, such as cyclones or hurricanes, may also displace great quantities of water, causing a high tide known as a storm surge that also resembles a tsunami.

TEKS Standard §112.16(b)(4)(B)

34. B: Goggles are proper protective eyewear for laboratory. Glasses provide almost no protection as they could break and they are open around the sides where chemicals could splash into the eyes. An eye wash is used to rinse out eyes if chemicals accidently get splashed into them.

TEKS Standard §112.16(b)(6)

35. B: The picture shows an arrow behind the box pushing it forward. If the box were being pulled, the arrow would be in front of the box pulling the box forward. Gravity pulls downward, not forward.

TEKS Standard §112.16(b)(1)(A)

36. D: Labeling beakers before adding fluids to them helps to ensure that the fluids are placed in correct containers and can be identified after being poured. Smelling, tasting, and adding chemicals other than those directed by your instructor are a violation of lab safety.

TEKS Standard §112.16(b)(5)

37. B: A spoiling apple has undergone a chemical change (one substance is changed into another). Dissolving both sand and salt in water, refers to a physical change, since the salt and water and the sand and water can be separated again by evaporating the water, which is a physical change. Pulverized rock is also an example of a physical change where the form has changed but not the substance itself.

TEKS Standard §112.16(b)(10)(A)
38. B: Polar bears, seals, and walrus' all live in arctic climates where it is very cold all year round. The thick layer of blubber that these animals have below the surface of their skin helps them preserve body heat keeping them warm in the frigid environment.

TEKS Standard §112.16(b)(1)(A)
39. B: Brushing hair is not a requirement after completing a laboratory assignment. Choice A, washing hands is required after every lab experiment in order to ensure that no chemicals or lab agents are ingested. Cleaning up the lab area ensures that all equipment is ready for the next experiment. Finishing the assignment is also necessary in order to draw a conclusion from the data collected.

TEKS Standard §112.16(b)(10)(A)
40. A: Cacti live in a desert environment where water is scarce. When it rains, cacti must be able to absorb and store as much water as possible so that they have water available during the dry periods. The folds on the outside of a cactus allow it to expand and fill with water. After a heavy rain, cacti will appear round and plump because the folds are full of water.

TEKS Standard §112.16(b)(8)
41. B: As the earth travels around the sun, it tilts towards the sun or away from it, depending on where it is in its orbit. This tilt is what determines the seasons. The earth is tilted towards the sun in summer and away from it in winter. Elevation a. and latitude c. of an area remain constant throughout the year, so they cannot account for the changing of the seasons. Air masses d. can influence the weather, but don't determine the seasons.

TEKS Standard §112.16(b)(1)(A)
42. A: Dispose of the solutions according to local disposal procedures. Solutions and compounds used in labs may be hazardous according to state and local regulatory agencies and should be treated with such precaution. Answer B, Empty the solutions into the sink and rinse with warm water and soap, does not take into account the hazards associated with a specific solution in terms of vapors, or interactions with water, soap and waste piping systems. Answer C, Ensure the solutions are secured in closed containers and throw away, may allow toxic chemicals to get into landfills and subsequently into fresh water systems. Answer D, Store the solutions in a secured, dry place for later use, is incorrect as chemicals should not be re-used due to the possibility of contamination.

TEKS Standard §112.16(b)(5)(B)
43. B: The freezing point of sea water is lower than fresh water as sea water is more dense. It is more dense because it has more dissolved salts. The freezing point changes with salinity, pressure and density, but can be -2°C (28.4°F) compared with fresh water, 0°C (32°F). As sea water freezes, it forms pockets of high-salinity brine that do not freeze. The brine slowly leaches out of the sea water ice as it forms. When the ice eventually melts, it has a lesser degree of salinity.

TEKS Standard §112.16(b)(7)(A)

44. D: The formation of sedimentary rock does not include heat. Of the three types of rock igneous, sedimentary and metamorphic, heat is essential to two: igneous and metamorphic. Sedimentary rocks are formed by sediments that get deposited and then compacted or cemented together. Sedimentary rocks are classified into detrital, organic or chemical sediments. Answer A, layering, is correct since sediments can be deposited or otherwise formed in layers. Answer B, cementation, is also called lithification. Answer C, compaction, refers to the pressure forming sedimentary rock leading to cementation.

Secret Key #1 - Time is Your Greatest Enemy

Pace Yourself

Wear a watch. At the beginning of the test, check the time (or start a chronometer on your watch to count the minutes), and check the time after every few questions to make sure you are "on schedule."

If you are forced to speed up, do it efficiently. Usually one or more answer choices can be eliminated without too much difficulty. Above all, don't panic. Don't speed up and just begin guessing at random choices. By pacing yourself, and continually monitoring your progress against your watch, you will always know exactly how far ahead or behind you are with your available time. If you find that you are one minute behind on the test, don't skip one question without spending any time on it, just to catch back up. Take 15 fewer seconds on the next four questions, and after four questions you'll have caught back up. Once you catch back up, you can continue working each problem at your normal pace.

Furthermore, don't dwell on the problems that you were rushed on. If a problem was taking up too much time and you made a hurried guess, it must be difficult. The difficult questions are the ones you are most likely to miss anyway, so it isn't a big loss. It is better to end with more time than you need than to run out of time.

Lastly, sometimes it is beneficial to slow down if you are constantly getting ahead of time. You are always more likely to catch a careless mistake by working more slowly than quickly, and among very high-scoring test takers (those who are likely to have lots of time left over), careless errors affect the score more than mastery of material.

Secret Key #2 - Guessing is not Guesswork

You probably know that guessing is a good idea - unlike other standardized tests, there is no penalty for getting a wrong answer. Even if you have no idea about a question, you still have a 20-25% chance of getting it right.

Most test takers do not understand the impact that proper guessing can have on their score. Unless you score extremely high, guessing will significantly contribute to your final score.

Monkeys Take the Test

What most test takers don't realize is that to insure that 20-25% chance, you have to guess randomly. If you put 20 monkeys in a room to take this test, assuming they answered once per question and behaved themselves, on average they would get 20-25% of the questions correct. Put 20 test takers in the room, and the average will be much lower among guessed questions. Why?
   1. The test writers intentionally write deceptive answer choices that "look" right. A test taker has no idea about a question, so picks the "best looking" answer, which is often

wrong. The monkey has no idea what looks good and what doesn't, so will consistently be lucky about 20-25% of the time.

2. Test takers will eliminate answer choices from the guessing pool based on a hunch or intuition. Simple but correct answers often get excluded, leaving a 0% chance of being correct. The monkey has no clue, and often gets lucky with the best choice.

This is why the process of elimination endorsed by most test courses is flawed and detrimental to your performance- test takers don't guess, they make an ignorant stab in the dark that is usually worse than random.

$5 Challenge

Let me introduce one of the most valuable ideas of this course- the $5 challenge:

You only mark your "best guess" if you are willing to bet $5 on it.
You only eliminate choices from guessing if you are willing to bet $5 on it.

Why $5? Five dollars is an amount of money that is small yet not insignificant, and can really add up fast (20 questions could cost you $100). Likewise, each answer choice on one question of the test will have a small impact on your overall score, but it can really add up to a lot of points in the end.

The process of elimination IS valuable. The following shows your chance of guessing it right:

If you eliminate wrong answer choices until only this many remain:	Chance of getting it correct:
1	100%
2	50%
3	33%

However, if you accidentally eliminate the right answer or go on a hunch for an incorrect answer, your chances drop dramatically: to 0%. By guessing among all the answer choices, you are GUARANTEED to have a shot at the right answer.

That's why the $5 test is so valuable- if you give up the advantage and safety of a pure guess, it had better be worth the risk.

What we still haven't covered is how to be sure that whatever guess you make is truly random. Here's the easiest way:

Always pick the first answer choice among those remaining.

Such a technique means that you have decided, **before you see a single test question**, exactly how you are going to guess- and since the order of choices tells you nothing about which one is correct, this guessing technique is perfectly random.

This section is not meant to scare you away from making educated guesses or eliminating choices- you just need to define when a choice is worth eliminating. The $5 test, along with a pre-defined random guessing strategy, is the best way to make sure you reap all of the benefits of guessing.

Secret Key #3 - Practice Smarter, Not Harder

Many test takers delay the test preparation process because they dread the awful amounts of practice time they think necessary to succeed on the test. We have refined an effective method that will take you only a fraction of the time.

There are a number of "obstacles" in your way to succeed. Among these are answering questions, finishing in time, and mastering test-taking strategies. All must be executed on the day of the test at peak performance, or your score will suffer. The test is a mental marathon that has a large impact on your future.

Just like a marathon runner, it is important to work your way up to the full challenge. So first you just worry about questions, and then time, and finally strategy:

Success Strategy

1. Find a good source for practice tests.
2. If you are willing to make a larger time investment, consider using more than one study guide- often the different approaches of multiple authors will help you "get" difficult concepts.
3. Take a practice test with no time constraints, with all study helps "open book." Take your time with questions and focus on applying strategies.
4. Take a practice test with time constraints, with all guides "open book."
5. Take a final practice test with no open material and time limits

If you have time to take more practice tests, just repeat step 5. By gradually exposing yourself to the full rigors of the test environment, you will condition your mind to the stress of test day and maximize your success.

Secret Key #4 - Prepare, Don't Procrastinate

Let me state an obvious fact: if you take the test three times, you will get three different scores. This is due to the way you feel on test day, the level of preparedness you have, and, despite the test writers' claims to the contrary, some tests WILL be easier for you than others.

Since your future depends so much on your score, you should maximize your chances of success. In order to maximize the likelihood of success, you've got to prepare in advance. This means taking practice tests and spending time learning the information and test taking strategies you will need to succeed.

Never take the test as a "practice" test, expecting that you can just take it again if you need to. Feel free to take sample tests on your own, but when you go to take the official test, be prepared, be focused, and do your best the first time!

Secret Key #5 - Test Yourself

Everyone knows that time is money. There is no need to spend too much of your time or too little of your time preparing for the test. You should only spend as much of your precious time preparing as is necessary for you to get the score you need.

Once you have taken a practice test under real conditions of time constraints, then you will know if you are ready for the test or not.

If you have scored extremely high the first time that you take the practice test, then there is not much point in spending countless hours studying. You are already there.

Benchmark your abilities by retaking practice tests and seeing how much you have improved. Once you score high enough to guarantee success, then you are ready.

If you have scored well below where you need, then knuckle down and begin studying in earnest. Check your improvement regularly through the use of practice tests under real conditions. Above all, don't worry, panic, or give up. The key is perseverance!

Then, when you go to take the test, remain confident and remember how well you did on the practice tests. If you can score high enough on a practice test, then you can do the same on the real thing.

General Strategies

The most important thing you can do is to ignore your fears and jump into the test immediately- do not be overwhelmed by any strange-sounding terms. You have to jump into the test like jumping into a pool- all at once is the easiest way.

Make Predictions

As you read and understand the question, try to guess what the answer will be. Remember that several of the answer choices are wrong, and once you begin reading them, your mind will immediately become cluttered with answer choices designed to throw you off. Your mind is typically the most focused immediately after you have read the question and digested its contents. If you can, try to predict what the correct answer will be. You may be surprised at what you can predict.

Quickly scan the choices and see if your prediction is in the listed answer choices. If it is, then you can be quite confident that you have the right answer. It still won't hurt to check the other answer choices, but most of the time, you've got it!

Answer the Question

It may seem obvious to only pick answer choices that answer the question, but the test writers can create some excellent answer choices that are wrong. Don't pick an answer just because it sounds right, or you believe it to be true. It MUST answer the question. Once you've made your selection, always go back and check it against the question and make sure that you didn't misread the question, and the answer choice does answer the question posed.

Benchmark

After you read the first answer choice, decide if you think it sounds correct or not. If it doesn't, move on to the next answer choice. If it does, mentally mark that answer choice. This doesn't mean that you've definitely selected it as your answer choice, it just means that it's the best you've seen thus far. Go ahead and read the next choice. If the next choice is worse than the one you've already selected, keep going to the next answer choice. If the next choice is better than the choice you've already selected, mentally mark the new answer choice as your best guess.

The first answer choice that you select becomes your standard. Every other answer choice must be benchmarked against that standard. That choice is correct until proven otherwise by another answer choice beating it out. Once you've decided that no other answer choice seems as good, do one final check to ensure that your answer choice answers the question posed.

Valid Information

Don't discount any of the information provided in the question. Every piece of information may be necessary to determine the correct answer. None of the information in the question is there to throw you off (while the answer choices will certainly have information to throw you off). If two seemingly unrelated topics are discussed, don't ignore either. You can be confident there is a relationship, or it wouldn't be included in the question, and you are probably going to have to determine what is that relationship to find the answer.

Avoid "Fact Traps"

Don't get distracted by a choice that is factually true. Your search is for the answer that answers the question. Stay focused and don't fall for an answer that is true but incorrect. Always go back to the question and make sure you're choosing an answer that actually answers the question and is not just a true statement. An answer can be factually correct, but it MUST answer the question asked. Additionally, two answers can both be seemingly correct, so be sure to read all of the answer choices, and make sure that you get the one that BEST answers the question.

Milk the Question

Some of the questions may throw you completely off. They might deal with a subject you have not been exposed to, or one that you haven't reviewed in years. While your lack of knowledge about the subject will be a hindrance, the question itself can give you many clues that will help you find the correct answer. Read the question carefully and look for clues. Watch particularly for adjectives and nouns describing difficult terms or words that you don't recognize. Regardless of if you completely understand a word or not, replacing it with a synonym either provided or one you more familiar with may help you to understand what the questions are asking. Rather than wracking your mind about specific detailed information concerning a difficult term or word, try to use mental substitutes that are easier to understand.

The Trap of Familiarity

Don't just choose a word because you recognize it. On difficult questions, you may not recognize a number of words in the answer choices. The test writers don't put "make-believe" words on the test; so don't think that just because you only recognize all the words in one answer choice means that answer choice must be correct. If you only recognize words in one answer choice, then focus on that one. Is it correct? Try your best to determine if it is correct. If it is, that is great, but if it doesn't, eliminate it. Each word and answer choice you eliminate increases your chances of getting the question correct, even if you then have to guess among the unfamiliar choices.

Eliminate Answers

Eliminate choices as soon as you realize they are wrong. But be careful! Make sure you consider all of the possible answer choices. Just because one appears right, doesn't mean that the next one won't be even better! The test writers will usually put more than one good answer choice for every question, so read all of them. Don't worry if you are stuck between two that seem right. By getting down to just two remaining possible choices, your odds are now 50/50. Rather than wasting too much time, play the odds. You are guessing, but guessing wisely, because you've been able to knock out some of the answer choices that you know are wrong. If you are eliminating choices and realize that the last answer choice you are left with is also obviously wrong, don't panic. Start over and consider each choice again. There may easily be something that you missed the first time and will realize on the second pass.

Tough Questions

If you are stumped on a problem or it appears too hard or too difficult, don't waste time. Move on! Remember though, if you can quickly check for obviously incorrect answer choices, your chances of guessing correctly are greatly improved. Before you completely give up, at least try to knock out a couple of possible answers. Eliminate what you can and then guess at the remaining answer choices before moving on.

Brainstorm

If you get stuck on a difficult question, spend a few seconds quickly brainstorming. Run through the complete list of possible answer choices. Look at each choice and ask yourself, "Could this answer the question satisfactorily?" Go through each answer choice and consider it independently of the other. By systematically going through all possibilities, you may find something that you would otherwise overlook. Remember that when you get stuck, it's important to try to keep moving.

Read Carefully

Understand the problem. Read the question and answer choices carefully. Don't miss the question because you misread the terms. You have plenty of time to read each question thoroughly and make sure you understand what is being asked. Yet a happy medium must be attained, so don't waste too much time. You must read carefully, but efficiently.

Face Value

When in doubt, use common sense. Always accept the situation in the problem at face value. Don't read too much into it. These problems will not require you to make huge leaps of logic. The test writers aren't trying to throw you off with a cheap trick. If you have to go beyond creativity and make a leap of logic in order to have an answer choice answer the question, then you should look at the other answer choices. Don't overcomplicate the problem by creating theoretical relationships or explanations that will warp time or space. These are normal problems rooted in reality. It's just that the applicable relationship or explanation may not be readily apparent and you have to figure things out. Use your common sense to interpret anything that isn't clear.

Prefixes

If you're having trouble with a word in the question or answer choices, try dissecting it. Take advantage of every clue that the word might include. Prefixes and suffixes can be a huge help. Usually they allow you to determine a basic meaning. Pre- means before, post- means after, pro - is positive, de- is negative. From these prefixes and suffixes, you can get an idea of the general meaning of the word and try to put it into context. Beware though of any traps. Just because con is the opposite of pro, doesn't necessarily mean congress is the opposite of progress!

Hedge Phrases

Watch out for critical "hedge" phrases, such as likely, may, can, will often, sometimes, often, almost, mostly, usually, generally, rarely, sometimes. Question writers insert these hedge phrases to cover every possibility. Often an answer choice will be wrong simply because it leaves no room for exception. Avoid answer choices that have definitive words like "exactly," and "always".

Switchback Words

Stay alert for "switchbacks". These are the words and phrases frequently used to alert you to shifts in thought. The most common switchback word is "but". Others include although, however, nevertheless, on the other hand, even though, while, in spite of, despite, regardless of.

New Information

Correct answer choices will rarely have completely new information included. Answer choices typically are straightforward reflections of the material asked about and will directly relate to the question. If a new piece of information is included in an answer choice that doesn't even seem to relate to the topic being asked about, then that answer choice is likely incorrect. All of the information needed to answer the question is usually provided for you, and so you should not have to make guesses that are unsupported or choose answer choices that require unknown information that cannot be reasoned on its own.

Time Management

On technical questions, don't get lost on the technical terms. Don't spend too much time on any one question. If you don't know what a term means, then since you don't have a dictionary, odds are you aren't going to get much further. You should immediately recognize terms as whether or not you know them. If you don't, work with the other clues that you have, the other answer choices and terms provided, but don't waste too much time trying to figure out a difficult term.

Contextual Clues

Look for contextual clues. An answer can be right but not correct. The contextual clues will help you find the answer that is most right and is correct. Understand the context in which a phrase or statement is made. This will help you make important distinctions.

Don't Panic

Panicking will not answer any questions for you. Therefore, it isn't helpful. When you first see the question, if your mind goes blank, take a deep breath. Force yourself to mechanically go through the steps of solving the problem and using the strategies you've learned.

Pace Yourself

Don't get clock fever. It's easy to be overwhelmed when you're looking at a page full of questions, your mind is full of random thoughts and feeling confused, and the clock is ticking down faster than you would like. Calm down and maintain the pace that you have set for yourself. As long as you are on track by monitoring your pace, you are guaranteed to have enough time for yourself. When you get to the last few minutes of the test, it may seem like you won't have enough time left, but if you only have as many questions as you should have left at that point, then you're right on track!

Answer Selection

The best way to pick an answer choice is to eliminate all of those that are wrong, until only one is left and confirm that is the correct answer. Sometimes though, an answer choice may immediately look right. Be careful! Take a second to make sure that the other choices are not equally obvious. Don't make a hasty mistake. There are only two times that you should stop before checking other answers. First is when you are positive that the answer choice you have selected is correct. Second is when time is almost out and you have to make a quick guess!

Check Your Work

Since you will probably not know every term listed and the answer to every question, it is important that you get credit for the ones that you do know. Don't miss any questions through careless mistakes. If at all possible, try to take a second to look back over your answer selection and make sure you've selected the correct answer choice and haven't made a costly careless mistake (such as marking an answer choice that you didn't mean to mark). This quick double check should more than pay for itself in caught mistakes for the time it costs.

Beware of Directly Quoted Answers

Sometimes an answer choice will repeat word for word a portion of the question or reference section. However, beware of such exact duplication – it may be a trap! More than likely, the correct choice will paraphrase or summarize a point, rather than being exactly the same wording.

Slang

Scientific sounding answers are better than slang ones. An answer choice that begins "To compare the outcomes..." is much more likely to be correct than one that begins "Because some people insisted..."

Extreme Statements

Avoid wild answers that throw out highly controversial ideas that are proclaimed as established fact. An answer choice that states the "process should be used in certain situations, if..." is much more likely to be correct than one that states the "process should be discontinued completely."   The first is a calm rational statement and doesn't even make a definitive, uncompromising stance, using a hedge word "if" to provide wiggle room, whereas the second choice is a radical idea and far more extreme.

Answer Choice Families

When you have two or more answer choices that are direct opposites or parallels, one of them is usually the correct answer.   For instance, if one answer choice states "x increases" and another answer choice states "x decreases" or "y increases," then those two or three answer choices are very similar in construction and fall into the same family of answer choices.   A family of answer choices is when two or three answer choices are very similar in construction, and yet often have a directly opposite meaning.   Usually the correct answer choice will be in that family of answer choices.   The "odd man out" or answer choice that doesn't seem to fit the parallel construction of the other answer choices is more likely to be incorrect.

Top 20 Test Taking Tips

1. Carefully follow all the test registration procedures
2. Know the test directions, duration, topics, question types, how many questions
3. Setup a flexible study schedule at least 3-4 weeks before test day
4. Study during the time of day you are most alert, relaxed, and stress free
5. Maximize your learning style; visual learner use visual study aids, auditory learner use auditory study aids
6. Focus on your weakest knowledge base
7. Find a study partner to review with and help clarify questions
8. Practice, practice, practice
9. Get a good night's sleep; don't try to cram the night before the test
10. Eat a well-balanced meal
11. Know the exact physical location of the testing site; drive the route to the site prior to test day
12. Bring a set of ear plugs; the testing center could be noisy
13. Wear comfortable, loose fitting, layered clothing to the testing center; prepare for it to be either cold or hot during the test
14. Bring at least 2 current forms of ID to the testing center
15. Arrive to the test early; be prepared to wait and be patient
16. Eliminate the obviously wrong answer choices, then guess the first remaining choice
17. Pace yourself; don't rush, but keep working and move on if you get stuck
18. Maintain a positive attitude even if the test is going poorly
19. Keep your first answer unless you are positive it is wrong
20. Check your work, don't make a careless mistake

Special Report: What Your Test Score Will Tell You About Your IQ

Did you know that most standardized tests correlate very strongly with IQ? In fact, your general intelligence is a better predictor of your success than any other factor, and most tests intentionally measure this trait to some degree to ensure that those selected by the test are truly qualified for the test's purposes.

Before we can delve into the relation between your test score and IQ, I will first have to explain what exactly is IQ. Here's the formula:

Your IQ = 100 + (Number of standard deviations below or above the average)*15

Now, let's define standard deviations by using an example. If we have 5 people with 5 different heights, then first we calculate the average. Let's say the average was 65 inches. The standard deviation is the "average distance" away from the average of each of the members. It is a direct measure of variability - if the 5 people included Jackie Chan and Shaquille O'Neal, obviously there's a lot more variability in that group than a group of 5 sisters who are all within 6 inches in height of each other. The standard deviation uses a number to characterize the average range of difference within a group.

A convenient feature of most groups is that they have a "normal" distribution- makes sense that most things would be normal, right? Without getting into a bunch of statistical mumbo-jumbo, you just need to know that if you know the average of the group and the standard deviation, you can successfully predict someone's percentile rank in the group.

Confused? Let me give you an example. If instead of 5 people's heights, we had 100 people, we could figure out their rank in height JUST by knowing the average, standard deviation, and their height. We wouldn't need to know each person's height and manually rank them, we could just predict their rank based on three numbers.

What this means is that you can take your PERCENTILE rank that is often given with your test and relate this to your RELATIVE IQ of people taking the test - that is, your IQ relative to the people taking the test. Obviously, there's no way to know your actual IQ because the people taking a standardized test are usually not very good samples of the general population- many of those with extremely low IQ's never achieve a level of success or competency necessary to complete a typical standardized test. In fact, professional psychologists who measure IQ actually have to use non-written tests that can fairly measure the IQ of those not able to complete a traditional test.

The bottom line is to not take your test score too seriously, but it is fun to compute your "relative IQ" among the people who took the test with you. I've done the calculations below. Just look up your percentile rank in the left and then you'll see your "relative IQ" for your test in the right hand column-

Percentile Rank	Your Relative IQ		Percentile Rank	Your Relative IQ
99	135		59	103
98	131		58	103
97	128		57	103
96	126		56	102
95	125		55	102
94	123		54	102
93	122		53	101
92	121		52	101
91	120		51	100
90	119		50	100
89	118		49	100
88	118		48	99
87	117		47	99
86	116		46	98
85	116		45	98
84	115		44	98
83	114		43	97
82	114		42	97
81	113		41	97
80	113		40	96
79	112		39	96
78	112		38	95
77	111		37	95
76	111		36	95
75	110		35	94
74	110		34	94
73	109		33	93
72	109		32	93
71	108		31	93
70	108		30	92
69	107		29	92
68	107		28	91
67	107		27	91
66	106		26	90
65	106		25	90
64	105		24	89
63	105		23	89
62	105		22	88
61	104		21	88
60	104		20	87

Special Report: What is Test Anxiety and How to Overcome It?

The very nature of tests caters to some level of anxiety, nervousness or tension, just as we feel for any important event that occurs in our lives. A little bit of anxiety or nervousness can be a good thing. It helps us with motivation, and makes achievement just that much sweeter. However, too much anxiety can be a problem; especially if it hinders our ability to function and perform.

"Test anxiety," is the term that refers to the emotional reactions that some test-takers experience when faced with a test or exam. Having a fear of testing and exams is based upon a rational fear, since the test-taker's performance can shape the course of an academic career. Nevertheless, experiencing excessive fear of examinations will only interfere with the test-takers ability to perform, and his/her chances to be successful.

There are a large variety of causes that can contribute to the development and sensation of test anxiety. These include, but are not limited to lack of performance and worrying about issues surrounding the test.

Lack of Preparation

Lack of preparation can be identified by the following behaviors or situations:

Not scheduling enough time to study, and therefore cramming the night before the test or exam
Managing time poorly, to create the sensation that there is not enough time to do everything
Failing to organize the text information in advance, so that the study material consists of the entire text and not simply the pertinent information
Poor overall studying habits

Worrying, on the other hand, can be related to both the test taker, or many other factors around him/her that will be affected by the results of the test. These include worrying about:

Previous performances on similar exams, or exams in general
How friends and other students are achieving
The negative consequences that will result from a poor grade or failure

There are three primary elements to test anxiety. Physical components, which involve the same typical bodily reactions as those to acute anxiety (to be discussed below). Emotional factors have to do with fear or panic. Mental or cognitive issues concerning attention spans and memory abilities.

Physical Signals

There are many different symptoms of test anxiety, and these are not limited to mental and emotional strain. Frequently there are a range of physical signals that will let a test taker know that he/she is suffering from test anxiety. These bodily changes can include the following:

Perspiring
Sweaty palms
Wet, trembling hands
Nausea
Dry mouth
A knot in the stomach
Headache
Faintness
Muscle tension
Aching shoulders, back and neck
Rapid heart beat
Feeling too hot/cold

To recognize the sensation of test anxiety, a test-taker should monitor him/herself for the following sensations:

The physical distress symptoms as listed above
Emotional sensitivity, expressing emotional feelings such as the need to cry or laugh too much, or a sensation of anger or helplessness
A decreased ability to think, causing the test-taker to blank out or have racing thoughts that are hard to organize or control.

Though most students will feel some level of anxiety when faced with a test or exam, the majority can cope with that anxiety and maintain it at a manageable level. However, those who cannot are faced with a very real and very serious condition, which can and should be controlled for the immeasurable benefit of this sufferer.

Naturally, these sensations lead to negative results for the testing experience. The most common effects of test anxiety have to do with nervousness and mental blocking.

Nervousness

Nervousness can appear in several different levels:

The test-taker's difficulty, or even inability to read and understand the questions on the test
The difficulty or inability to organize thoughts to a coherent form
The difficulty or inability to recall key words and concepts relating to the testing questions (especially essays)
The receipt of poor grades on a test, though the test material was well known by the test taker

Conversely, a person may also experience mental blocking, which involves:

Blanking out on test questions
Only remembering the correct answers to the questions when the test has already finished.

Fortunately for test anxiety sufferers, beating these feelings, to a large degree, has to do with proper preparation. When a test taker has a feeling of preparedness, then anxiety will be dramatically lessened.

The first step to resolving anxiety issues is to distinguish which of the two types of anxiety are being suffered. If the anxiety is a direct result of a lack of preparation, this should be considered a normal reaction, and the anxiety level (as opposed to the test results) shouldn't be anything to worry about. However, if, when adequately prepared, the test-taker still panics, blanks out, or seems to overreact, this is not a fully rational reaction. While this can be considered normal too, there are many ways to combat and overcome these effects.

Remember that anxiety cannot be entirely eliminated, however, there are ways to minimize it, to make the anxiety easier to manage. Preparation is one of the best ways to minimize test anxiety. Therefore the following techniques are wise in order to best fight off any anxiety that may want to build.

To begin with, try to avoid cramming before a test, whenever it is possible. By trying to memorize an entire term's worth of information in one day, you'll be shocking your system, and not giving yourself a very good chance to absorb the information. This is an easy path to anxiety, so for those who suffer from test anxiety, cramming should not even be considered an option.

Instead of cramming, work throughout the semester to combine all of the material which is presented throughout the semester, and work on it gradually as the course goes by, making sure to master the main concepts first, leaving minor details for a week or so before the test.

To study for the upcoming exam, be sure to pose questions that may be on the examination, to gauge the ability to answer them by integrating the ideas from your texts, notes and lectures, as well as any supplementary readings.

If it is truly impossible to cover all of the information that was covered in that particular term, concentrate on the most important portions, that can be covered very well. Learn these concepts as best as possible, so that when the test comes, a goal can be made to use these concepts as presentations of your knowledge.

In addition to study habits, changes in attitude are critical to beating a struggle with test anxiety. In fact, an improvement of the perspective over the entire test-taking experience can actually help a test taker to enjoy studying and therefore improve the overall experience. Be certain not to overemphasize the significance of the grade - know that the result of the test is neither a reflection of self worth, nor is it a measure of intelligence; one grade will not predict a person's future success.

To improve an overall testing outlook, the following steps should be tried:

Keeping in mind that the most reasonable expectation for taking a test is to expect to try to demonstrate as much of what you know as you possibly can.
Reminding ourselves that a test is only one test; this is not the only one, and there will be others.
The thought of thinking of oneself in an irrational, all-or-nothing term should be avoided at all costs.
A reward should be designated for after the test, so there's something to look forward to. Whether it be going to a movie, going out to eat, or simply visiting friends, schedule it in advance, and do it no matter what result is expected on the exam.

Test-takers should also keep in mind that the basics are some of the most important things, even beyond anti-anxiety techniques and studying. Never neglect the basic social, emotional and biological needs, in order to try to absorb information. In order to best achieve, these three factors must be held as just as important as the studying itself.

Study Steps

Remember the following important steps for studying:

Maintain healthy nutrition and exercise habits. Continue both your recreational activities and social pass times. These both contribute to your physical and emotional wellbeing.
Be certain to get a good amount of sleep, especially the night before the test, because when you're overtired you are not able to perform to the best of your best ability.
Keep the studying pace to a moderate level by taking breaks when they are needed, and varying the work whenever possible, to keep the mind fresh instead of getting bored.
When enough studying has been done that all the material that can be learned has been learned, and the test taker is prepared for the test, stop studying and do something relaxing such as listening to music, watching a movie, or taking a warm bubble bath.

There are also many other techniques to minimize the uneasiness or apprehension that is experienced along with test anxiety before, during, or even after the examination. In fact, there are a great deal of things that can be done to stop anxiety from interfering with lifestyle and performance. Again, remember that anxiety will not be eliminated entirely, and it shouldn't be. Otherwise that "up" feeling for exams would not exist, and most of us depend on that sensation to perform better than usual. However, this anxiety has to be at a level that is manageable.

Of course, as we have just discussed, being prepared for the exam is half the battle right away. Attending all classes, finding out what knowledge will be expected on the exam, and knowing the exam schedules are easy steps to lowering anxiety. Keeping up with work will remove the need to cram, and efficient study habits will eliminate wasted time. Studying should be done in an ideal location for concentration, so that it is simple to become interested in the material and give it complete attention. A method such as SQ3R (Survey, Question, Read, Recite, Review) is a wonderful key to follow to make sure that the study habits are as effective as possible, especially in the case of learning from a textbook. Flashcards are great techniques for memorization. Learning to take good notes will mean that notes will be full of useful information, so that less sifting will need to be done to seek out what is pertinent for studying. Reviewing notes after class and then again on occasion will keep the information fresh in the mind. From notes that have been taken summary sheets and outlines can be made for simpler reviewing.

A study group can also be a very motivational and helpful place to study, as there will be a sharing of ideas, all of the minds can work together, to make sure that everyone understands, and the studying will be made more interesting because it will be a social occasion.

Basically, though, as long as the test-taker remains organized and self confident, with efficient study habits, less time will need to be spent studying, and higher grades will be achieved.

To become self confident, there are many useful steps. The first of these is "self talk." It has been shown through extensive research, that self-talk for students who suffer from test anxiety, should be well monitored, in order to make sure that it contributes to self confidence as opposed to sinking the student. Frequently the self talk of test-anxious students is negative or self-defeating, thinking that everyone else is smarter and faster, that they always mess up, and that if they don't do well, they'll fail the entire course. It is important to decreasing anxiety that awareness is made of self talk. Try writing any negative self thoughts and then disputing them with a positive statement instead. Begin self-encouragement as though it was a friend speaking. Repeat positive statements to help reprogram the mind to believing in successes instead of failures.

Helpful Techniques

Other extremely helpful techniques include:

Self-visualization of doing well and reaching goals
While aiming for an "A" level of understanding, don't try to "overprotect" by setting your expectations lower. This will only convince the mind to stop studying in order to meet the lower expectations.
Don't make comparisons with the results or habits of other students. These are individual factors, and different things work for different people, causing different results.
Strive to become an expert in learning what works well, and what can be done in order to improve. Consider collecting this data in a journal.
Create rewards for after studying instead of doing things before studying that will only turn into avoidance behaviors.
Make a practice of relaxing - by using methods such as progressive relaxation, self-hypnosis, guided imagery, etc - in order to make relaxation an automatic sensation.
Work on creating a state of relaxed concentration so that concentrating will take on the focus of the mind, so that none will be wasted on worrying.
Take good care of the physical self by eating well and getting enough sleep.
Plan in time for exercise and stick to this plan.

Beyond these techniques, there are other methods to be used before, during and after the test that will help the test-taker perform well in addition to overcoming anxiety.

Before the exam comes the academic preparation. This involves establishing a study schedule and beginning at least one week before the actual date of the test. By doing this, the anxiety of not having enough time to study for the test will be automatically eliminated. Moreover, this will make the studying a much more effective experience, ensuring that the learning will be an easier process. This relieves much undue pressure on the test-taker.

Summary sheets, note cards, and flash cards with the main concepts and examples of these main concepts should be prepared in advance of the actual studying time. A topic should never be eliminated from this process. By omitting a topic because it isn't expected to be on the test is only setting up the test-taker for anxiety should it actually appear on the exam. Utilize the course syllabus for laying out the topics that should be studied. Carefully go over the notes that were made in class, paying special attention to any of the issues that the professor took special care to emphasize while lecturing in class. In the textbooks, use the chapter review, or if possible, the chapter tests, to begin your review.

It may even be possible to ask the instructor what information will be covered on the exam, or what the format of the exam will be (for example, multiple choice, essay, free form, true-false). Additionally, see if it is possible to find out how many questions will be on the test. If a review sheet or sample test has been offered by the professor, make good use of it, above anything else, for the preparation for the test. Another great resource for getting to know the examination is reviewing tests from previous semesters. Use these tests to review, and aim to achieve a 100% score on each of the possible topics. With a few exceptions, the goal that you set for yourself is the highest one that you will reach.

Take all of the questions that were assigned as homework, and rework them to any other possible course material. The more problems reworked, the more skill and confidence will form as a result. When forming the solution to a problem, write out each of the steps. Don't simply do head work. By doing as many steps on paper as possible, much clarification and therefore confidence will be formed. Do this with as many homework problems as possible, before checking the answers. By checking the answer after each problem, a reinforcement will exist, that will not be on the exam. Study situations should be as exam-like as possible, to prime the test-taker's system for the experience. By waiting to check the answers at the end, a psychological advantage will be formed, to decrease the stress factor.

Another fantastic reason for not cramming is the avoidance of confusion in concepts, especially when it comes to mathematics. 8-10 hours of study will become one hundred percent more effective if it is spread out over a week or at least several days, instead of doing it all in one sitting. Recognize that the human brain requires time in order to assimilate new material, so frequent breaks and a span of study time over several days will be much more beneficial.

Additionally, don't study right up until the point of the exam. Studying should stop a minimum of one hour before the exam begins. This allows the brain to rest and put things in their proper order. This will also provide the time to become as relaxed as possible when going into the examination room. The test-taker will also have time to eat well and eat sensibly. Know that the brain needs food as much as the rest of the body. With enough food and enough sleep, as well as a relaxed attitude, the body and the mind are primed for success.

Avoid any anxious classmates who are talking about the exam. These students only spread anxiety, and are not worth sharing the anxious sentimentalities.

Before the test also involves creating a positive attitude, so mental preparation should also be a point of concentration. There are many keys to creating a positive attitude. Should fears become rushing in, make a visualization of taking the exam, doing well, and seeing an A written on the paper. Write out a list of affirmations that will bring a feeling of confidence, such as "I am doing well in my English class," "I studied well and know my material," "I enjoy this class." Even if the affirmations aren't believed at first, it sends a positive message to the subconscious which will result in an alteration of the overall belief system, which is the system that creates reality.

If a sensation of panic begins, work with the fear and imagine the very worst! Work through the entire scenario of not passing the test, failing the entire course, and dropping out of school, followed by not getting a job, and pushing a shopping cart through the dark alley where you'll live. This will place things into perspective! Then, practice deep breathing and create a visualization of the opposite situation - achieving an "A" on the exam, passing the entire course, receiving the degree at a graduation ceremony.

On the day of the test, there are many things to be done to ensure the best results, as well as the most calm outlook. The following stages are suggested in order to maximize test-taking potential:

Begin the examination day with a moderate breakfast, and avoid any coffee or beverages with caffeine if the test taker is prone to jitters. Even people who are used to managing caffeine can feel jittery or light-headed when it is taken on a test day.
Attempt to do something that is relaxing before the examination begins. As last minute cramming clouds the mastering of overall concepts, it is better to use this time to create a calming outlook.
Be certain to arrive at the test location well in advance, in order to provide time to select a location that is away from doors, windows and other distractions, as well as giving enough time to relax before the test begins.
Keep away from anxiety generating classmates who will upset the sensation of stability and relaxation that is being attempted before the exam.
Should the waiting period before the exam begins cause anxiety, create a self-distraction by reading a light magazine or something else that is relaxing and simple.

During the exam itself, read the entire exam from beginning to end, and find out how much time should be allotted to each individual problem. Once writing the exam, should more time be taken for a problem, it should be abandoned, in order to begin another problem. If there is time at the end, the unfinished problem can always be returned to and completed.

Read the instructions very carefully - twice - so that unpleasant surprises won't follow during or after the exam has ended.

When writing the exam, pretend that the situation is actually simply the completion of homework within a library, or at home. This will assist in forming a relaxed atmosphere, and will allow the brain extra focus for the complex thinking function.

Begin the exam with all of the questions with which the most confidence is felt. This will build the confidence level regarding the entire exam and will begin a quality momentum. This will also create encouragement for trying the problems where uncertainty resides.

Going with the "gut instinct" is always the way to go when solving a problem. Second guessing should be avoided at all costs. Have confidence in the ability to do well.

For essay questions, create an outline in advance that will keep the mind organized and make certain that all of the points are remembered. For multiple choice, read every answer, even if the correct one has been spotted - a better one may exist.

Continue at a pace that is reasonable and not rushed, in order to be able to work carefully. Provide enough time to go over the answers at the end, to check for small errors that can be corrected.

Should a feeling of panic begin, breathe deeply, and think of the feeling of the body releasing sand through its pores. Visualize a calm, peaceful place, and include all of the sights, sounds and sensations of this image. Continue the deep breathing, and take a few minutes to continue this with closed eyes. When all is well again, return to the test.

If a "blanking" occurs for a certain question, skip it and move on to the next question. There will be time to return to the other question later. Get everything done that can be done, first, to guarantee all the grades that can be compiled, and to build all of the confidence possible. Then return to the weaker questions to build the marks from there.

Remember, one's own reality can be created, so as long as the belief is there, success will follow. And remember: anxiety can happen later, right now, there's an exam to be written!

After the examination is complete, whether there is a feeling for a good grade or a bad grade, don't dwell on the exam, and be certain to follow through on the reward that was promised...and enjoy it! Don't dwell on any mistakes that have been made, as there is nothing that can be done at this point anyway.

Additionally, don't begin to study for the next test right away. Do something relaxing for a while, and let the mind relax and prepare itself to begin absorbing information again.

From the results of the exam - both the grade and the entire experience, be certain to learn from what has gone on. Perfect studying habits and work some more on confidence in order to make the next examination experience even better than the last one.

Learn to avoid places where openings occurred for laziness, procrastination and day dreaming.

Use the time between this exam and the next one to better learn to relax, even learning to relax on cue, so that any anxiety can be controlled during the next exam. Learn how to relax the body. Slouch in your chair if that helps. Tighten and then relax all of the different muscle groups, one group at a time, beginning with the feet and then working all the way up to the neck and face. This will ultimately relax the muscles more than they were to begin with. Learn how to breathe deeply and comfortably, and focus on this breathing going in and out as a relaxing thought. With every exhale, repeat the word "relax."

As common as test anxiety is, it is very possible to overcome it. Make yourself one of the test-takers who overcome this frustrating hindrance.

Special Report: Retaking the Test: What Are Your Chances at Improving Your Score?

After going through the experience of taking a major test, many test takers feel that once is enough. The test usually comes during a period of transition in the test taker's life, and taking the test is only one of a series of important events. With so many distractions and conflicting recommendations, it may be difficult for a test taker to rationally determine whether or not he should retake the test after viewing his scores.

The importance of the test usually only adds to the burden of the retake decision. However, don't be swayed by emotion. There a few simple questions that you can ask yourself to guide you as you try to determine whether a retake would improve your score:

1. What went wrong? Why wasn't your score what you expected?

Can you point to a single factor or problem that you feel caused the low score? Were you sick on test day? Was there an emotional upheaval in your life that caused a distraction? Were you late for the test or not able to use the full time allotment? If you can point to any of these specific, individual problems, then a retake should definitely be considered.

2. Is there enough time to improve?

Many problems that may show up in your score report may take a lot of time for improvement. A deficiency in a particular math skill may require weeks or months of tutoring and studying to improve. If you have enough time to improve an identified weakness, then a retake should definitely be considered.

3. How will additional scores be used? Will a score average, highest score, or most recent score be used?

Different test scores may be handled completely differently. If you've taken the test multiple times, sometimes your highest score is used, sometimes your average score is computed and used, and sometimes your most recent score is used. Make sure you understand what method will be used to evaluate your scores, and use that to help you determine whether a retake should be considered.

4. Are my practice test scores significantly higher than my actual test score?

If you have taken a lot of practice tests and are consistently scoring at a much higher level than your actual test score, then you should consider a retake. However, if you've taken five practice tests and only one of your scores was higher than your actual test score, or if your practice test scores were only slightly higher than your actual test score, then it is unlikely that you will significantly increase your score.

5. Do I need perfect scores or will I be able to live with this score? Will this score still allow me to follow my dreams?

What kind of score is acceptable to you? Is your current score "good enough?" Do you have to have a certain score in order to pursue the future of your dreams? If you won't be happy with your current score, and there's no way that you could live with it, then you should consider a retake. However, don't get your hopes up. If you are looking for significant improvement, that may or may not be possible. But if you won't be happy otherwise, it is at least worth the effort.

Remember that there are other considerations. To achieve your dream, it is likely that your grades may also be taken into account. A great test score is usually not the only thing necessary to succeed. Make sure that you aren't overemphasizing the importance of a high test score.

Furthermore, a retake does not always result in a higher score. Some test takers will score lower on a retake, rather than higher. One study shows that one-fourth of test takers will achieve a significant improvement in test score, while one-sixth of test takers will actually show a decrease. While this shows that most test takers will improve, the majority will only improve their scores a little and a retake may not be worth the test taker's effort.

Finally, if a test is taken only once and is considered in the added context of good grades on the part of a test taker, the person reviewing the grades and scores may be tempted to assume that the test taker just had a bad day while taking the test, and may discount the low test score in favor of the high grades. But if the test is retaken and the scores are approximately the same, then the validity of the low scores are only confirmed. Therefore, a retake could actually hurt a test taker by definitely bracketing a test taker's score ability to a limited range.

Special Report: Additional Bonus Material

Due to our efforts to try to keep this book to a manageable length, we've created a link that will give you access to all of your additional bonus material.

Please visit http://www.mometrix.com/bonus948/staarg5sci to access the information.